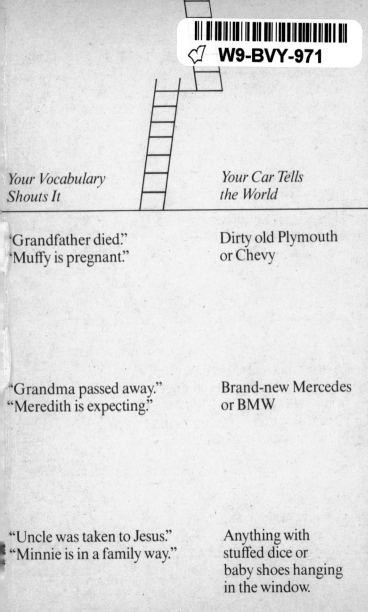

Your Vocabulary Shouts It	Your Car Tells the World
'Grandfather died." 'Muffy is pregnant."	Dirty old Plymouth or Chevy
"Grandma passed away." "Meredith is expecting."	Brand-new Mercedes or BMW
"Uncle was taken to Jesus." "Minnie is in a family way."	Anything with stuffed dice or baby shoes hanging in the window.

(Please turn the page for rave reviews of CLASS.)

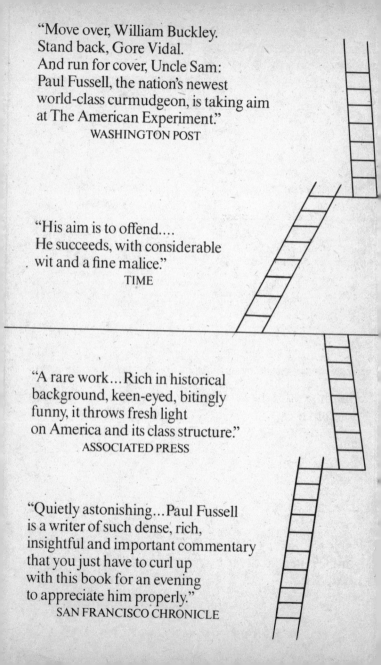

CLASS

Paul Fussell

BALLANTINE BOOKS • NEW YORK

Library of Congress Catalog Card Number: 83-12637

ISBN 0-345-31816-1

This edition published by arrangement with Summit Books

Manufactured in the United States of America

First Ballantine Books Edition: October 1984
Twelfth Printing: June 1989

ACKNOWLEDGMENTS

I am grateful to the many people who have interested themselves in this project or who have—sometimes inadvertently—supplied me with data. Especially helpful have been James Anderson, Jack Beatty, Jake Blumenthal, Henry E. Bradshaw, Alfred Bush, Edward T. Cone, Theodore and Mary Cross, Kit Davies, Ira and Judy Davis, Eileen Fallon, Betty Fussell, Angeline Goreau, John Hutchinson, David Johnson, Patrick J. and Marian Kelleher, Michael Kinsley, Fletcher and Laura Berquist Knebel, Don Kowet, A. Walton Litz, Donald and Fleury Mackie, Anthony Manousos, Edgar Mayhew, Joyce Carol Oates, George Pitcher, Miles Rind, James Silberman, Claude M. Spilman, Jr., Brian Stratton, Rod Townley, and Alan Williams. During work on this book I have enjoyed the friendship of Harriette Behringer and John Scanlan. I want to thank both for their generosity.

To
Tucky and Sam

Contents

I	A Touchy Subject	1
II	An Anatomy of the Classes	12
III	Appearance Counts	47
IV	About the House	80
V	Consumption, Recreation, *Bibelots*	107
VI	The Life of the Mind	146
VII	"Speak, That I May See Thee"	175
VIII	Climbing and Sinking, and Prole Drift	200
IX	The X Way Out	212
	Appendix: Exercises, and the Mail Bag	225

※] 1 [※

A TOUCHY SUBJECT

ALTHOUGH MOST AMERICANS SENSE THAT THEY LIVE within an extremely complicated system of social classes and suspect that much of what is thought and done here is prompted by considerations of status, the subject has remained murky. And always touchy. You can outrage people today simply by mentioning social class, very much the way, sipping tea among the aspidistras a century ago, you could silence a party by adverting too openly to sex. When, recently, asked what I am writing, I have answered, "A book about social class in America," people tend first to straighten their ties and sneak a glance at their cuffs to see how far fraying has advanced there. Then, a few minutes later, they silently get up and walk away. It is not just that I am feared as a class spy. It is as if I had said, "I am working on a book urging the beating to death of baby whales using the dead bodies of baby seals." Since I have been writing this book I have experienced many times the awful truth of R. H. Tawney's perception, in his book *Equality* (1931): "The word 'class' is fraught with unpleasing associations, so that to linger upon it is apt to be interpreted as the symptom of a

1

perverted mind and a jaundiced spirit."

Especially in America, where the idea of class is notably embarrassing. In his book *Inequality in an Age of Decline* (1980), the sociologist Paul Blumberg goes so far as to call it "America's forbidden thought." Indeed, people often blow their tops if the subject is even broached. One woman, asked by a couple of interviewers if she thought there were social classes in this country, answered: "It's the dirtiest thing I've ever heard of!" And a man, asked the same question, got so angry that he blurted out, "Social class should be exterminated!"

Actually, you reveal a great deal about your social class by the amount of annoyance or fury you feel when the subject is brought up. A tendency to get very anxious suggests that you are middle-class and nervous about slipping down a rung or two. On the other hand, upper-class people love the topic to come up: the more attention paid to the matter the better off they seem to be. Proletarians generally don't mind discussions of the subject because they know they can do little to alter their class identity. Thus the whole class matter is likely to seem like a joke to them—the upper classes fatuous in their empty aristocratic pretentiousness, the middles loathsome in their anxious gentility. It is the middle class that is highly class-sensitive, and sometimes class-scared to death. A representative of that class left his mark on a library copy of Russell Lynes's *The Tastemakers* (1954). Next to a passage patronizing the insecure decorating taste of the middle class and satirically contrasting its artistic behavior to that of some more sophisticated classes, this offended reader scrawled, in large capitals, "BULL SHIT!" A hopelessly middle-class man (not a woman, surely?) if I ever saw one.

If you reveal your class by your outrage at the very

topic, you reveal it also by the way you define the thing that's outraging you. At the bottom, people tend to believe that class is defined by the amount of money you have. In the middle, people grant that money has something to do with it, but think education and the kind of work you do almost equally important. Nearer the top, people perceive that taste, values, ideas, style, and behavior are indispensable criteria of class, regardless of money or occupation or education. One woman interviewed by Studs Terkel for *Division Street: America* (1967) clearly revealed her class as middle both by her uneasiness about the subject's being introduced and by her instinctive recourse to occupation as the essential class criterion. "We have right on this street almost every class," she said. "But I shouldn't say class," she went on, "because we don't live in a nation of classes." Then, the occupational criterion: "But we have janitors living on the street, we have doctors, we have businessmen, CPAs."

Being told that there are no social classes in the place where the interviewee lives is an old experience for sociologists. "'We don't have classes in our town' almost invariably is the first remark recorded by the investigator," reports Leonard Reissman, author of *Class in American Life* (1959). "Once that has been uttered and is out of the way, the class divisions in the town can be recorded with what seems to be an amaz-degree of agreement among the good citizens of the community." The novelist John O'Hara made a whole career out of probing into this touchy subject, to which he was astonishingly sensitive. While still a boy, he was noticing that in the Pennsylvania town where he grew up, "older people do not treat others as equals."

Class distinctions in America are so complicated and subtle that foreign visitors often miss the nuances and sometimes even the existence of a class structure. So powerful is "the fable of equality," as Frances Trollope called it when she toured America in 1832, so embarrassed is the government to confront the subject—in the thousands of measurements pouring from its bureaus, social class is not officially recognized—that it's easy for visitors not to notice the way the class system works. A case in point is the experience of Walter Allen, the British novelist and literary critic. Before he came over here to teach at a college in the 1950s, he imagined that "class scarcely existed in America, except, perhaps, as divisions between ethnic groups or successive waves of immigrants." But living awhile in Grand Rapids opened his eyes: there he learned of the snob power of New England and the pliability of the locals to the long-wielded moral and cultural authority of old families.

Some Americans viewed with satisfaction the failure of the 1970s TV series *Beacon Hill*, a drama of high society modeled on the British *Upstairs, Downstairs*, comforting themselves with the belief that this venture came to grief because there is no class system here to sustain interest in it. But they were mistaken. *Beacon Hill* failed to engage American viewers because it focused on perhaps the least interesting place in the indigenous class structure, the quasi-aristocratic upper class. Such a dramatization might have done better if it had dealt with places where everyone recognizes interesting class collisions occur—the place where the upper-middle class meets the middle and resists its attempted incursions upward, or where the middle class does the same to the classes just below it.

If foreigners often fall for the official propaganda of social equality, the locals tend to know what's what, even if they feel some uneasiness talking about it. When the acute black from the South asserts of an ambitious friend that "Joe can't class with the big folks," we feel in the presence of someone who's attended to actuality. Like the carpenter who says: "I hate to say there are classes, but it's just that people are more comfortable with people of like backgrounds." His grouping of people by "like backgrounds," scientifically uncertain as it may be, is nearly as good a way as any to specify what it is that distinguishes one class from another. If you feel no need to explicate your allusions or in any way explain what you mean, you are probably talking with someone in your class. And that's true whether you're discussing the Rams and the Forty-Niners, RVs, the House (i.e., Christ Church, Oxford), Mama Leone's, the Big Board, "the Vineyard," "Baja," or the Porcellian.

In this book I am going to deal with some of the visible and audible signs of social class, but I will be sticking largely with those that reflect choice. That means that I will not be considering matters of race, or, except now and then, religion or politics. Race is visible, but it is not chosen. Religion and politics, while usually chosen, don't show, except for the occasional front-yard shrine or car bumper sticker. When you look at a person you don't see "Roman Catholic" or "liberal": you see "hand-painted necktie" or "crappy polyester shirt"; you hear *parameters* or *in regards to*. In attempting to make sense of indicators like these, I have been guided by perception and feel rather than by any method that could be deemed "scientific," believing with Arthur Marwick, author of *Class: Image and Reality* (1980), that "class . . . is too serious a subject to leave to the social scientists."

It should be a serious subject in America especially, because here we lack a convenient system of inherited titles, ranks, and honors, and each generation has to define the hierarchies all over again. The society changes faster than any other on earth, and the American, almost uniquely, can be puzzled about where, in the society, he stands. The things that conferred class in the 1930s—white linen golf knickers, chrome cocktail shakers, vests with white piping—are, to put it mildly, unlikely to do so today. Belonging to a rapidly changing rather than a traditional society, Americans find Knowing Where You Stand harder than do most Europeans. And a yet more pressing matter, Making It, assumes crucial importance here. "How'm I doin'?" Mayor Koch of New York used to bellow, and most of his audience sensed that he was, appropriately, asking the representative American question.

It seems no accident that, as the British philosopher Anthony Quinton says, "The book of etiquette in its modern form...is largely an American product, the great names being Emily Post...and Amy Vanderbilt." The reason is that the United States is preeminently the venue of newcomers, with a special need to place themselves advantageously and to get on briskly. "Some newcomers," says Quinton, "are geographical, that is, im.nigrants; others are economic, the newly rich; others again chronological, the young." All are faced with the problem inseparable from the operations of a mass society, earning respect. The comic Rodney Dangerfield, complaining that he don't get none, belongs to the same national species as that studied by John Adams, who says, as early as 1805: "The rewards...in this life are *esteem* and *admiration* of others—the punishments are *neglect* and *contempt*....The desire of the esteem of others is as real a want of nature as hunger—and the neglect and contempt of the world as severe a pain as the gout or stone...." About the same time the Irish poet Thomas Moore, sensing the special predicament Americans were inviting with their egalitarian Constitution, described the citizens of Washington, D.C., as creatures

Born to be slaves, and struggling to be lords.

Thirty years later, in *Democracy in America*, Alexis de Tocqueville put his finger precisely on the special problem of class aspiration here. "Nowhere," he wrote, "do citizens appear so insignificant as in a democratic nation." Nowhere, consequently, is there more strenuous effort to achieve—*earn* would probably not be the right word—significance. And still later in the nineteenth century, Walt Whitman, in *Democratic Vistas* (1871), perceived that in the United States, where the form of government promotes a condition (or at least an illusion) of uniformity among the citizens, one of the unique anxieties is going to be the constant struggle for individual self-respect based upon social approval. That is, where everybody is somebody, nobody is anybody. In a recent Louis Harris poll, "respect from others" is what 76 percent of respondents said they wanted most. Addressing prospective purchasers of a coffee table, an ad writer recently spread before them this most enticing American vision: "Create a rich, warm, sensual allusion to your own good taste that will demand respect and consideration in every setting you care to imagine."

The special hazards attending the class situation in America, where movement appears so fluid and where the prizes seem available to anyone who's lucky, are disappointment, and, following close on that, envy. Because the myth conveys the impression that you can readily earn your way upward, disillusion and bitterness are particularly strong when you find yourself trapped in a class system you've been half persuaded isn't important. When in early middle life some people discover that certain limits have been placed on their capacity to ascend socially by such apparent irrelevancies as heredity, early environment, and the social class of their immediate forebears, they go into something like despair, which, if generally secret, is no less destructive.

De Tocqueville perceived the psychic dangers. "In democratic times," he granted, "enjoyments are more intense than in the ages of aristocracy, and the number of those who partake in them is vastly larger." But, he added, in egalitarian atmospheres "man's hopes and desires are oftener blasted, the soul is more stricken and perturbed, and care itself more keen."

And after blasted hopes, envy. The force of sheer class envy behind vile and even criminal behavior in this country, the result in part of disillusion over the official myth of classlessness, should never be underestimated. The person who, parking his attractive car in a large city, has returned to find his windows smashed and his radio aerial snapped off will understand what I mean. Speaking in West Virginia in 1950, Senator Joseph R. McCarthy used language that leaves little doubt about what he was really getting at—not so much "Communism" as the envied upper-middle and upper classes. "It has not been the less fortunate or members of minority groups who have been selling this nation out," he said, "but rather those who have had all the benefits . . . , the finest homes, the finest college education. . . ." Pushed far enough, class envy issues in revenge egalitarianism, which the humorist Roger Price, in *The Great Roob Revolution* (1970), distinguishes from "democracy" thus: "Democracy demands that all of its citizens begin the race even. Egalitarianism insists that they all *finish* even." Then we get the situation satirized in L. P. Hartley's novel *Facial Justice* (1960), about "the prejudice against good looks" in a future society somewhat like ours. There, inequalities of appearance are redressed by government plastic surgeons, but the scalpel isn't used to make everyone beautiful—it's used to make everyone plain.

* * *

Despite our public embrace of political and judicial equality, in individual perception and understanding—much of which we refrain from publicizing—we arrange things vertically and insist on crucial differences in value. Regardless of what we say about equality, I think everyone at some point comes to feel like the Oscar Wilde who said, "The brotherhood of man is not a mere poet's dream: it is a most depressing and humiliating reality." It's as if in our heart of hearts we don't want agglomerations but distinctions. Analysis and separation we find interesting, synthesis boring.

Although it is disinclined to designate a hierarchy of social classes, the federal government seems to admit that if in law we are all equal, in virtually all other ways we are not. Thus the eighteen grades into which it divides its civil-service employees, from grade 1 at the bottom (messenger, etc.) up through 2 (mail clerk), 5 (secretary), 9 (chemist), to 14 (legal administrator), and finally 16, 17, and 18 (high-level administrators). In the construction business there's a social hierarchy of jobs, with "dirt work," or mere excavation, at the bottom; the making of sewers, roads, and tunnels in the middle; and work on buildings (the taller, the higher) at the top. Those who sell "executive desks" and related office furniture know that they and their clients agree on a rigid "class" hierarchy. Desks made of oak are at the bottom, and those of walnut are next. Then, moving up, mahogany is, if you like, "upper-middle class," until we arrive, finally, at the apex: teak. In the army, at ladies' social functions, pouring the coffee is the prerogative of the senior officer's wife because, as the ladies all know, coffee outranks tea.

There seems no place where hierarchical status-orderings aren't discoverable. Take musical instru-

U.S. ARMY SCENE: A SENIOR OFFICER'S WIFE (NOTE
PSEUDO-UPPER-MIDDLE-CLASS GETUP) POURS COFFEE
INTO CUPS OF SUBORDINATES' WIVES

ments. In a symphony orchestra the customary ranking
of sections recognizes the difficulty and degree of subtlety of various kinds of instruments: strings are on
top, woodwinds just below, then brass, and, at the
bottom, percussion. On the difficulty scale, the ac-
cordion is near the bottom, violin near the top. Another
way of assigning something like "social class" to instruments is to consider the prestige of the group in
which the instrument is customarily played. As the
composer Edward T. Cone says, "If you play a violin,
you can play in a string quartet or symphony orchestra,
but not in a jazz band and certainly not in a marching
band. Among woodwinds, therefore, flute, and oboe,
which are primarily symphonic instruments, are 'better' than the clarinet, which can be symphonic, jazz,
or band. Among brasses, the French horn ranks highest
because it hasn't customarily been used in jazz. Among

percussionists, tympani is high for the same reason." And (except for the bassoon) the lower the notes an instrument is designed to produce, in general the lower its class, bass instruments being generally easier to play. Thus a sousaphone is lower than a trumpet, a bass viol lower than a viola, etc. If you hear "My boy's taking lessons on the trombone," your smile will be a little harder to control than if you hear "My boy's taking lessons on the flute." On the other hand, to hear "My boy's taking lessons on the viola da gamba" is to receive a powerful signal of class, the kind attaching to antiquarianism and museum, gallery, or "educational" work. Guitars (except when played in "classical"—that is, archaic—style) are low by nature, and that is why they were so often employed as tools of intentional class degradation by young people in the 1960s and '70s. The guitar was the perfect instrument for the purpose of signaling these young people's flight from the upper-middle and middle classes, associated as it is with Gypsies, cowhands, and other personnel without inherited or often even earned money and without fixed residence.

The former Socialist and editor of the *Partisan Review* William Barrett, looking back thirty years, concludes that "the Classless Society looks more and more like a Utopian illusion. The socialist countries develop a class structure of their own," although there, he points out, the classes are very largely based on bureaucratic toadying. "Since we are bound...to have classes in any case, why not have them in the more organic, heterogeneous and variegated fashion" indigenous to the West? And since we have them, why not know as much as we can about them? The subject may be touchy, but it need not be murky forever.

AN ANATOMY OF THE CLASSES

NOBODY KNOWS FOR SURE WHAT THE WORD *CLASS* means. Some people, like Vance Packard, have tried to invoke more objective terms, and have spoken about *status systems*. Followers of the sociologist Max Weber tend to say *class* when they're talking about the amount of money you have and the kind of leverage it gives you; they say *status* when they mean your social prestige in relation to your audience; and they say *party* when they're measuring how much political power you have, that is, how much built-in resistance you have to being pushed around by shits. By *class* I mean all three, with perhaps extra emphasis on *status*. I do wish the word *caste* were domesticated in the United States, because it nicely conveys the actual rigidity of class lines here, the difficulty of moving—either upward or downward—out of the place where you were nurtured.

How many classes are there? The simplest answer is that there are only two, the rich and the poor, employer and employed, landlord and tenant, bourgeois and proletariat. Or, to consider manners rather than economics and politics, there are gentlemen and there are cads. Asked by a team of sociologists what's involved in "social class," one respondent said, "Whether you have couth or are uncouth." And there's a "social" division distinguishing those who "entertain" in their domestic premises and those who wouldn't think of it. Paul Blumberg notes "a fundamental class cleavage" today between people who can afford to buy a house—any house—and people who can't, a fairly elevated version of the distinction down below between those who own cars and those who must depend on public transportation and who thus spend a great deal of their time waiting around for the bus to show up. In her book *Class* (1981), British humorist Jilly Cooper suggests a bipartite social scene in which the two parties are the Guilty and the Cross:

> On the one side are the middle and upper classes, feeling guilty and riddled with social concern although they often earn less money than the workers. On the other are the working classes, who have been totally brainwashed by television and magazine images of the good life, and feel cross because they aren't getting a big enough slice of the cake.

Two classes only were in the consciousness of the British Eighth Army infantryman in North Africa during the Second World War who delivered this eloquent account of them:

> Sir, this is a fine way for a man to spend his fucking life, isn't it? Have you ever heard of class distinction, sir? I'll tell you what it means, it means Vickers-Armstrong booking a profit to look like a loss, and Churchill lighting a new cigar, and the *Times* explaining Liberty and Democracy, and me sitting on my arse in Libya splashing a fainting man with water out of my steel helmet. It's a very fine thing if only you're in the right class—that's highly important,

sir, because one class gets the sugar and the other class gets the shit.

A way of bringing home that soldier's conclusion is to realize that all work everywhere is divided into two sorts, safe and dangerous. Every year 100,000 workers are killed or die of work-related accidents or disease; 400,000 are disabled; 6 million are hurt at work. In *The Working-Class Majority* (1974), Andrew Levison says, "All the clichés and pleasant notions of how the old class divisions...have disappeared are exposed as hollow phrases by the simple fact that American workers must accept serious injury and even death as part of their daily reality while the middle class does not." And he goes on:

> Imagine...the universal outcry that would occur if every year several corporate headquarters routinely collapsed like mines, crushing sixty or seventy executives. Or suppose that all the banks were filled with an invisible noxious dust that constantly produced cancer in the managers, clerks, and tellers. Finally, try to imagine the horror...if thousands of university professors were deafened every year or lost fingers, hands, sometimes eyes, while on their jobs.

And speaking of death and injury, probably the most awful class division in America, one that cuts deeply across the center of society and that will poison life here for generations, is the one separating those whose young people were killed or savaged in the Vietnam War and those who, thanks largely to the infamous S-2 deferment for college students, escaped. Anyone uncertain about class consciousness in this country should listen to a working-class father whose son was killed:

> I'm bitter. You bet your goddam dollar I'm bitter. It's people like us who give up our sons for the

country. The business people, they run the country and make money from it. The college types, the professors, they go to Washington and tell the government what to do.... But their sons, they don't end up in the swamps over there, in Vietnam. No, sir.

And a mother adds: "We can't understand how all those rich kids—the kids with beads from the suburbs—how they get off when my son had to go."

The two-part division has the convenience of simplicity as well as usefulness in highlighting injustice and registering bitterness. A three-part division is popular too, probably because the number three is portentous, folkloristic, and even magical, being the number of bears, wishes, and Wise Men. In Britain three has been popularly accepted as the number of classes at least since the last century, when Matthew Arnold divided his neighbors and friends into upper, middle, and lower classes, or, as he memorably termed them, Barbarians (at the top, notice), Philistines (in the middle), and Populace. This three-tiered conception is the usual way to think of the class system for people in the middle, for it offers them moral and social safety, positioning them equally distant from the vices of pride and snobbery and waste and carelessness, which they associate with those above them, and dirtiness, constraint, and shame, the attendants of those below. Upper, middle, and lower are the customary terms for these three groups, although the British euphemism *working class* for *lower class* is now making some headway here.

If the popular number of classes is three, the number sociologists seem to favor is five:

> Upper
> Upper middle
> Middle

Lower middle
Lower

And trying to count the classes, some people simply give up, finding, like John Brooks in *Showing Off in America* (1981), that "in the new American structure there seem to be an almost infinite number of classes," or like the man in Boston asked about class there who said, "You have too many classes for me to count and name.... Hell! There may be fifteen or thirty." (He then added, like a good American, "Anyway, it doesn't matter a damn to me.")

My researches have persuaded me that there are nine classes in this country, as follows:

Top out-of-sight
Upper
Upper middle
———————

Middle
High proletarian
Mid-proletarian
Low proletarian
———————

Destitute
Bottom out-of-sight

One thing to get clear at the outset is this: it's not riches alone that defines these classes. "It can't be money," one working man says quite correctly, "because nobody ever knows that about you for sure." Style and taste and awareness are as important as money. "Economically, no doubt, there are only two classes, the rich and the poor," says George Orwell, "but socially there is a whole hierarchy of classes, and the manners and traditions learned by each class in childhood are not only very different but—this is the essential point—generally persist from birth to death.... It is...very difficult to escape, culturally, from the class into which you have been born." When John Fitzgerald Kennedy, watching Richard Nixon on television, turned to his friends and, horror-struck, said, "The guy has no class," he was not talking about money.

Anyone who imagines that large assets or high income confer high class can take comfort from a little book titled *Live a Year with a Millionaire*, written by Cornelius Vanderbilt Whitney and distributed by him (free) to his friends for Christmas 1981. Not to put too fine a point on it, the banality, stupidity, complacency, and witlessness of this author can remind a reader only of characters in Ring Lardner or in such satires by Sinclair Lewis as *The Man Who Knew Coolidge*. "They are a cosmopolitan group," says Whitney of people he meets at one party. "Come from places all over the States." The more he goes on, the more his reader will perceive that, except for his money, Whitney is a profoundly middle-class fellow, committed without any self-awareness to every cliché of that social rank.

And down below, the principle still holds: money doesn't matter that much. To illustrate the point, John Brooks compares two families living in adjoining houses in a suburb. One man is "blue-collar," a garage mechanic. The other is "white-collar," an employee in a publishing house. They make roughly the same amount of money, but what a difference. "Mr. Blue" bought a small, neat "ranch house." "Mr. White" bought a beat-up old house and refurbished it himself. Mrs. Blue uses the local shops, especially those in the nearby shopping center, and thinks them wonderful, "so convenient." Mrs. White goes to the city to buy her clothes. The Blues drink, but rather furtively, and usually on Saturday night with the curtains closed. The Whites drink openly, often right out in the backyard. "The Blues shout to each other, from room to room of their house or from corner to corner of their lot, without self-consciousness; the Whites modulate their voices to the point where they sometimes can't hear each other." As household objects, books are a crucial criterion. There's not a book in the Blues' house, while the Whites' living room contains numerous full book-shelves. Brooks concludes: "Here, in sum, are two families with hardly anything in common..., yet their...incomes are practically identical." Likewise, it was Russell Lynes's awareness that it's less money than taste and knowledge and perceptiveness that determine class that some years ago prompted him to set forth the tripartite scheme of *highbrow*, *middlebrow*, and *lowbrow*.

Not that the three classes at the top don't have money. The point is that money alone doesn't define them, for the *way* they have their money is largely

A HIGH PROLE REGARDING A DESTITUTE WITH DISDAIN, BUT LESS FOR HIS POVERTY THAN FOR HIS STYLE

what matters. That is, as a class indicator the amount of money is less significant than the source. The main thing distinguishing the top three classes from each other is the amount of money inherited in relation to the amount currently earned. The top-out-of-sight class (Rockefellers, Pews, DuPonts, Mellons, Fords, Vanderbilts) lives on inherited capital entirely. No one whose money, no matter how copious, comes from his own work—film stars are an example—can be a member of the top-out-of-sight class, even if the size of his income and the extravagance of his expenditure permit him to simulate identity with it. Inheritance—"old money" in the vulgar phrase—is the indispensable principle defining the top three classes, and it's best if the money's been in the family for three or four generations. There are subtle local ways to ascertain how long the money's been there. Touring middle America, the British traveler Jonathan Raban came upon the girl Sally, who informed him that "New Money says Missouri; Old Money says Missoura."

"When I think of a really rich man," says a Boston blue-collar, "I think of one of those estates where you can't see the house from the road." Hence the name of the top class, which could just as well be called "the class in hiding." Their houses are never seen from the street or road. They like to hide away deep in the hills or way off on Greek or Caribbean islands (which they tend to own), safe, for the moment, from envy and its ultimate attendants, confiscatory taxation and finally expropriation. It was the Great Depression, Vance Packard speculates, that badly frightened the very rich, teaching them to be "discreet, almost reticent, in exhibiting their wealth." From the 1930s dates the flight of money from such exhibitionistic venues as the mansions of upper Fifth Avenue to hideaways in Virginia, upper New York State, Connecticut, Long Island, and

New Jersey. The situation now is very different from the one in the 1890s satirized by Thorstein Veblen in *The Theory of the Leisure Class*. In his day the rich delighted to exhibit themselves conspicuously, with costly retainers and attendants much in evidence. Now they hide, not merely from envy and revenge but from exposé journalism, much advanced in cunning and ferocity since Veblen's time, and from an even worse threat, virtually unknown to Veblen, foundation mendicancy, with its hordes of beggars in three-piece suits constantly badgering the well-to-do. Showing off used to be the main satisfaction of being very rich in America. Now the rich must skulk and hide. It's a pity.

And it's not just that the individual houses and often the persons of the top-out-of-sights are removed from scrutiny. Their very class tends to escape the down-to-earth calculations of sociologists and poll-takers and consumer researchers. It's not studied because it's literally out of sight, and a questionnaire proffered to a top-out-of-sight person will very likely be hurled to the floor with disdain. Very much, in fact, the way it would be ignored by a bottom-out-of-sight person. And it's here that we begin to perceive one of the most wonderful things about the American class system—the curious similarity, if not actual brotherhood, of the top- and bottom-out-of-sights. Just as the tops are hidden away on their islands or behind the peek-a-boo walls of their distant estates, the bottoms are equally invisible, when not put away in institutions or claustrated in monasteries, lamaseries, or communes, then hiding from creditors, deceived bail-bondsmen, and gulled merchants intent on repossessing cars and furniture. (This bottom-out-of-sight class is visible briefly at one place and time, muttering its wayward fancies on the streets of New York in the spring. But after this ritual yearly show of itself it retreats into invisibility again.)

In aid of invisibility, members of both classes feel an equal anxiety to keep their names out of the papers. And the bottoms—"the lower or spurious leisure class," Veblen calls them—share something more with the top-out-of-sights. They do not earn their money. They are given it and kept afloat not by their own efforts or merits but by the welfare machinery or the correctional system, the way the tops owe it all to their ancestors. And a further similarity: members of both classes carry very little cash on their persons. We can say, in summary, that the virtual identity, in important respects, of top- and bottom-out-of-sights is a remarkable example of the time-proven principle that Extremes Meet.

The next class down, the upper class, differs from the top-out-of-sight class in two main ways. First, although it inherits a lot of its money, it earns quite a bit too, usually from some attractive, if slight, work, without which it would feel bored and even ashamed. It's likely to make its money by controlling banks and the more historic corporations, think tanks, and foundations, and to busy itself with things like the older universities, the Council on Foreign Relations, the Foreign Policy Association, the Committee for Economic Development, and the like, together with the executive branch of the federal government, and often the Senate. In the days when ambassadors were amateurs, they were selected largely from this class, very seldom from the top-out-of-sight. And secondly, unlike the top-out-of-sights, the upper class is visible, often ostentatiously so. Which is to say that the top-out-of-sights have spun off and away from Veblen's scheme of conspicuous exhibition, leaving the mere upper class to carry on its former role. When you pass a house with a would-be impressive façade visible from the street or highway, you know it's occupied by a member of the upper class. The White House is probably the

best example. Its residents, even on those occasions
when they are Franklin D. Roosevelts or even John F.
Kennedys, can never be designated top-out-of-sight
but only upper-class. The house is simply too showy,
being pure white and carefully positioned on high
ground, and temporary residence there usually con-
stitutes a come-down for most of its occupants. It is a
hopelessly upper-class place—or even lower than that,
as when the Harry Trumans lived there.

Of course no person is located within one of these
class categories exclusively. Consider William Ran-
dolph Hearst and his establishment at San Simeon. The
location is in a way top-out-of-sight, for the "house"
isn't visible from the highway, the nearest public access. But the façade of the main building, once you
penetrate through the miles of outdoor park and "zoo,"
is designed to evoke respect, or rather awe, in the
breast of the apprehender, and that indicates how very
un-top-out-of-sight Hearst remained despite his pseudo-
aristocratic airs. He cared too much what effect he was
having on people. His using paper napkins at his sump-
tuous and pretentious dinner parties is a promising sign
of a genuine aristocratic eccentricity, but his care that
his place should look impressive from the front—it
looks like the Cathedral of Avila, among other similar
structures—gives him away. Merely upper-middle-class
stumbling around in a boy's understanding of showing
off.

Like all the classes, the upper class has its distinct
stigmata. It will be in the *Social Register*, for example,
whereas the mere upper-middle class will not be, although it will slaver to get in. Having streets named
after you is a signal that you are probably upper-class.
At least if the street name's your surname: if it's your
first name (like *Kathy Street*), you are middle-class or
worse. Speaking French fluently, even though French

is irrelevant to one's actual life, business, interests, and the like, is an upper-class sign, although it's important not to speak it with anything resembling a correct, or "French," accent.

Not smoking at all is very upper-class, but in any way calling attention to one's abstinence drops one to middle-class immediately. The constant coming and going of "houseguests" is an all but infallible upper-class sign, implying as it does plenty of spare bedrooms to lodge them in and no anxiety about making them happy, what with all the drinks, food, games, parties, etc. It is among members of the upper class that you have to refrain from uttering compliments, which are taken to be rude, possessions there being of course beautiful, expensive, and impressive, without question. The paying of compliments is a middle-class convention, for this class needs the assurance compliments provide. In the upper class there's never any doubt of one's value, and it all goes without saying. A British peer of a very old family was once visited by an artistic young man who, entering the dining room, declared that he'd never seen a finer set of Hepplewhite chairs. His host had him ejected instantly, explaining, "Fellow praised my chairs! Damned cheek!" Dining among the uppers, one does not normally praise the food, because it goes without saying that the hostess would put forth nothing short of excellent. Besides, she's not cooked it. Likewise, if you spill a glass of wine, don't fret: the staff will clean it up.

Although not an infallible sign, because the upper-middle class has learned to ape it, devotion to horses—owning them, breeding them, riding them, racing them, chasing small animals while sitting on them—is, the way backgammon was before it became popular and lost caste, a fairly trustworthy upper-class mark. But it is, finally, by a characteristic the American upper class shares with all aristocracies that ye shall know them: their imperviousness to ideas and their total lack of interest in them. (A mark of the top-out-of-sights too, as Cornelius Vanderbilt Whitney's literary performance attests.) Their inattention to ideas is why Matthew Arnold calls them Barbarians, and he imputes their serenity specifically to their "never having had any ideas to trouble them." Still, they are a nice class, and the life among them is comfortable and ample and even entertaining, so long as you don't mind never hearing anyone saying anything intelligent or original.

We now come to the upper-middle class. It may possess virtually as much as the two classes above it. The difference is that it has earned most of it, in law, medicine, oil, shipping, real estate, or even the more honorific kinds of trade, like buying and selling works of art. Although they may enjoy some inherited money and use inherited "things" (silver, Oriental rugs), the upper-middles suffer from a bourgeois sense of shame, a conviction that to live on the earnings of others, even forebears, is not quite nice.

Caste marks of the upper-middles would include living in a house with more rooms than you need, except perhaps when a lot of "overnight guests" are present to help you imitate upper-class style. Another sign of the upper-middle class is its chastity in sexual display: the bathing suits affected by the women here are the most sexless in the world, Britain and Canada included. They feature boy-pants legs, in imitation of the boxer shorts favored by upper-middle-class men. Both men's and women's clothes here are designed to conceal, rather than underline, anatomical differences between the sexes. Hence, because men's shoulders constitute a secondary sexual characteristic, the natural-shoulder jacket. Epaulets emphasize the shoulders. They are thus associated with the lower classes, whose shoulders are required for physical work. The military makes much of epaulets, betraying instantly its prole associations. If you know someone who voted for John Anderson at the last presidential election, ten to one she's (or he's) upper-middle. This class is also the most "role-reversed" of all: men think nothing of cooking and doing housework, women of working out of the house in journalism, the theater, or real estate. (If the wife stays home all the time, the family's middle-class only.) Upper-middles like to show off their costly educations by naming their cats Spinoza, Clytemnestra, and Candide, which means, as you'll have inferred already, that it's in large part the class depicted in Lisa Birnbach and others' *Official Preppy Handbook*, that significantly popular artifact of 1980.

And it is the class celebrated also in the 1970 Ivy-idyllic film *Love Story*. The vast popularity of these two products suggests the appeal of the upper-middle style to all Americans who don't possess it. Indeed, most people of the middle classes and below would rather be in the upper-middle class than even the upper or the top-out-of-sight. A recent Louis Harris poll showed that when asked what class they'd like to be in, most said the middle class, and when asked what *part* of the middle class they'd like to be in, most said the upper-middle class. Being in the upper-middle class is a familiar and credible fantasy: its usages, while slightly grander than one's own, are recognizable and compassable, whereas in the higher classes you might be embarrassed by not knowing how to eat caviar or use a finger bowl or discourse in French. It's a rare American who doesn't secretly want to be upper-middle class.

We could gather as much, if in a coarser way, from a glance at two books by John T. Molloy, *Dress for Success* (1975) and *Molloy's Live for Success* (1981).

Molloy, whose talents are not at all contemptible, designates himself "America's first wardrobe engineer," in which capacity he is hired by businesses to advise them on principles of corporate dress. The ideal is for everyone in business to look upper-middle-class, because upper-middle-class equals Success. As he puts it with significant parallelism, "Successful dress is really no more than achieving good taste and the look of the upper-middle class." Even executives' offices can be tinkered with until they too emit an air of habitual success, which means, as Molloy says, that "the successful office exudes the qualities of the upper-middle class." That is, "It is (or looks) spacious and uncrowded. It is rich. It is well kept. It is tasteful. It is impressive. It is comfortable. It is private." And the waiting room too: it, "like the rest of your office, must immediately spell 'upper-middle class' to every visitor."

For Molloy, it's not just people's clothes and offices and waiting rooms that can be cosmeticized toward the upper-middle look. It's their faces, bodies, gestures, and postures as well. In *Molloy's Live for Success*, by the aid of line drawings he distinguishes between the male profile of the prole and the male profile of the upper-middle-class. The prole either has his jaw set in bitterness and defiance or his mouth open in doltish wonder. The upper-middle-class male, on the other hand, has his mouth closed but not too firmly set, and his shoulders avoid the hangdog, whip-me-again-master slouch Molloy finds characteristic of the unsuccessful. "Upper-middle-class and lower-middle-class people not only stand and sit differently," Molloy points out, "they move differently. Upper-middle-class people tend to have controlled precise movements. The way they use their arms and where their feet fall is dramatically different from lower-middle-class people, who tend to swing their arms out rather than hold them in closer to their bodies."

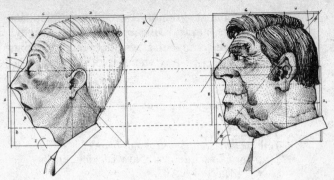

UPPER-MIDDLE AND PROLE PROFILES
(AFTER MOLLOY)

There's little doubt that instructors like Molloy—
and Michael Korda, author of *Success! How Every
Man and Woman Can Achieve It* (1975)—can teach
aspirants to simulate the upper-middle look. It's less
certain that they can ever teach what goes with it and
might be understood to cause it, the upper-middle-class
sense of relaxation, play, and, to a degree, irony. In
any other class we can imagine people contriving euphemisms for "Let's fuck." We can imagine, indeed,
members of any other class coming up with the colorful
invitation "Let's hide the salami." But it's unlikely that
any but the upper-middle class would say, as *The Official Preppy Handbook* records, "Let's *play* hide the
salami" and then affectionately abbreviate *salami* to
salam', the way it abbreviates Bloody Marys to Bloodys
and gin and tonics to G&Ts. It's all a game (in fact,
"the game of life") with the upper-middle class, and
hence its natural leaning toward frivolities like golf and
tennis and yachting. Who wouldn't want to be in a
class so free, secure, and amusing?

Before proceeding downward from these three top
classes, we must pause to consider the importance of

geographical place in defining them. People from the middle and prole classes will be tempted to imagine that place has little to do with class, that you can belong to the top classes just anywhere. Nothing could be more wrong.

("I understand, young man, that you want to join the Cosmopolitan Club."

"Yes, sir."

"Tell me, where do you come from?"

"Truth or Consequences, New Mexico, sir."

"I see." [*Averts eyes.*])

There are tens of thousands of places in the United States grand enough to have earned a Zip Code number. Given sufficient knowledge and a fine taste, it would be possible to rank them all according to their varying degrees of class, from Grosse Point and Watch Hill down to Needles and Pikesville. The best places socially would probably be found to be those longest under occupation by financially prudent Anglo-Saxons, like Newport, Rhode Island; Haddam, Connecticut; and Bar Harbor, Maine. Los Angeles would rank low less because it's ugly and banal than because it was owned by the Spanish for so long. A similar fact explains why St. Louis outranks San Antonio, Texas.

It's ultimately impossible to specify exactly what gives a place class. Fifty years ago H. L. Mencken, in *The American Mercury*, tried to create a trustworthy gauge by developing a hundred "social indicators" like the number of people in a given place who are listed in *Who's Who*, or who subscribe to *The Atlantic*, or who use up lots of gasoline. Today one would probably want to rank well up there a place that has experienced no dramatic increase in population since Mencken's time. This, at least, we can infer as a criterion from the fact that since 1940, the population of so awful a

place as Miami has increased from 172,000 to 343,000;
of Phoenix, from 65,000 to 683,000; and of San Diego,
from 200,000 to 840,000. Another sign of class desirability might be the absence of facilities for bowling.
I say that because Richard Boyer and David Savageau,
in their *Places Rated Almanac* (1981), have found that
the following places provide the best access to bowling
alleys, and we can't fail to note what regrettable places
they are:

> Billings, Montana
> Owensboro, Kentucky
> Midland, Texas
> Peoria, Illinois
> Dubuque, Iowa
> Odessa, Texas
> Alexandria, Louisiana

As I've just shown, it's probably easier to tell what
makes a place socially impossible than to indicate why
it's desirable. Another way to estimate a place's un-
desirability is to measure the degree to which religious
fundamentalism is identified with it. Akron, Ohio (a
dump, to be sure, by other criteria), is fatally known
as the home of the Rex Humbard Ministry, the way
Greenville, South Carolina, is known as the seat of
Bob Jones University, and Wheaton, Illinois, is identified with Wheaton College and remembered thus as
the forcing ground of the great Billy Graham. Likewise
Garden Grove, California, locus of the Rev. Robert
Schuller, famous for his automatic smile and his cheer-
ful Cathedral of Glass. Can a higher-class person live
in Lynchburg, Virginia? Probably not, since that town
is the origin of Dr. Jerry Falwell's radio emissions, the
site of his church, and the mailing address for free-will
offerings. Indeed, it seems a general principle that no
high-class person can live in any place associated with

religious prophecy or miracle, like Mecca, Bethlehem, Fatima, Lourdes, or Salt Lake City. It's notable that the most civilized places—London, Paris, Antibes, and even New York—pass safely through this test, although by the strictest application of the rule, Rome is a little doubtful. Still, classier than Jerusalem.

One signal of desirability is the quality of a city's best newspaper. The class inferiority of Washington, despite all its pretenses to high status, with its embassies and all, can be sensed the minute you open the *Washington Post*, which on Sunday provides its readers (high proles?) with not just a horoscope but lengthy plot summaries of the TV soaps, together with the advice of Ann Landers. In the same way, you can infer that Indianapolis carries little class clout by noticing that the *Indianapolis Star* offers its readers all these features, plus "Today's Prayer" on the front page. Both Florida (except perhaps for Palm Beach) and Southern California (except perhaps for Pasadena) have been considered socially disastrous for decades. As if the facts were well known, the vilest nightclubs abroad, especially in gotten-up new places like West Germany, are likely to be named Florida. One reason no civilized person could think of living near Tampa is that during the 1970s this sign was visible there, advertising nearby Apollo Beach: "Guy Lombardo Wants You as a Neighbor." In the same way, retired persons are solicited to share some of the magic of their musical hero by buying into the Lawrence Welk Country Club Mobile Estates in Escondido, California. In the classified section of a recent issue of the prole *National Enquirer* there were four ads offering fraudulent university degrees: all four listed California addresses. And some events seem class perfect: how right that the derelict *Queen Mary* should end as a piece of junk in precisely so witless a place as Long Beach, California, or that St. Petersburg, Florida, should find itself the site of the Dali Museum, or that Fort Lauderdale should be the headquarters of the STP Corporation.

In the face of this, the question arises, "Where then may a member of the top classes live in this country?" New York first of all, of course. Chicago. San Francisco. Philadelphia. Baltimore. Boston. Perhaps Cleveland. And deep in the countryside of Connecticut, New York State, Virginia, North Carolina, Pennsylvania, and Massachusetts. That's about it. It's not considered good form to live in New Jersey, except in Bernardsville and perhaps Princeton, but any place in New Jersey beats Sunnyvale, Cypress, and Compton, California; Canton, Ohio; Reno, Nevada; Cheyenne, Wyoming; Albuquerque, New Mexico; Columbus, Georgia, and similar Army towns; and Parma, Ohio, a city of 100,000 without a daily newspaper, bus system, hotel, or map of itself. Impossible also are Evergreen, Colorado, because John Hinckley came from there, and Dallas, because—among many other good reasons—Lee Harvey Oswald lived there. It is said that experts on the subject regard Las Vegas as "the world capital of tacky," and I suppose you could get some idea of the height of your social class by your lack of familiarity with it. And Acapulco as well?

Back, now, to the classes. The middle class is distinguishable more by its earnestness and psychic insecurity than by its middle income. I have known some very rich people who remain stubbornly middle-class, which is to say they remain terrified at what others think of them, and to avoid criticism are obsessed with doing everything right. The middle class is the place where table manners assume an awful importance and where net curtains flourish to conceal activities like hiding the salam' (a phrase no middle-class person would indulge in, surely: the fatuous *making love* is the middle-class equivalent). The middle class, always anxious about offending, is the main market for "mouthwashes," and if it disappeared the whole "deodorant" business would fall to the ground. If physicians tend to be upper-middle-class, dentists are gloomily aware that they're middle, and are said to experience frightful status anxieties when introduced socially to "physicians"—as dentists like to call them. (Physicians call themselves *doctors*, and enjoy doing this in front of dentists, as well as college professors, chiropractors, and divines.)

"Status panic": that's the affliction of the middle class, according to C. Wright Mills, author of *White Collar* (1951) and *The Power Elite* (1956). Hence the middles' need to accumulate credit cards and take in *The New Yorker*, which it imagines registers upper-middle taste. Its devotion to that magazine, or its ads, is a good example of Mills's description of the middle class as the one that tends "to borrow status from higher elements." *New Yorker* advertisers have always known this about their audience, and some of their pseudo-upper-middle gestures in front of the middles are hilarious, like one recently flogging expensive stationery, here, a printed invitation card. The pretentious Anglophile spelling of the second word strikes the right opening note:

In honour of
Dr and Mrs Leonard Adam Westman,
Dr and Mrs Jeffrey Logan Brandon
request the pleasure of your company for
[at this point the higher classes might say *cocktails*, or, if thoroughly secure, *drinks*. But here, "Dr." and Mrs. Brandon are inviting you to consume specifically—]

Champagne and Caviar
on Friday, etc., etc.

Valley Hunt Club,
Stamford, Conn., etc.

The only thing missing is the brand names of the refreshments.

If the audience for that sort of thing used to seem the most deeply rooted in time and place, today it seems the class that's the most rootless. Members of the middle class are not only the sort of people who buy their own heirlooms, silver, etc. They're also the people who do most of the moving long-distance (generally to very unstylish places), commanded every few years to pull up stakes by the corporations they're in bondage to. They are the geologist employed by the oil company, the computer programmer, the aeronautical engineer, the salesman assigned a new territory, and the "marketing" (formerly *sales*) manager deputed to keep an eye on him. These people and their families occupy the suburbs and developments. Their "Army and Navy," as William H. Whyte, Jr., says, is their corporate employer. IBM and DuPont hire these people from second-rate colleges and teach them that they are nothing if not members of the team. Virtually no latitude is permitted to individuality or the milder forms of eccentricity, and these employees soon learn to avoid all ideological statements, notably, as we'll see, in the furnishing of their living rooms. Terrified of losing their jobs, these people grow passive, their humanity diminished as they perceive themselves mere parts of an infinitely larger structure. And interchangeable parts, too. "The training makes our men interchangeable," an IBM executive was once heard to say.

It's little wonder that, treated like slaves most of the time, the middle class lusts for the illusion of weight and consequence. One sign is their quest for heraldic validation ("This beautiful embossed certificate will show your family tree"). Another is their custom of issuing annual family newsletters announcing the most recent triumphs in the race to become "professional":

John, who is now 22, is in his first year at the Dental School of Wayne State University.
Caroline has a fine position as an executive secretary for a prestigious firm in Boise, Idaho.

Sometimes these letters really wring the heart, with their proud lists of new "affiliations" achieved during the past year: "This year Bob became a member of the Junior Chamber of Commerce, the Beer Can Collectors League of North America, the Alumni Council of the University of Evansville, and the Young Republicans of Vanderburgh County." (Cf. Veblen: "Since conservatism is a characteristic of the wealthier and therefore more reputable portion of the community, it has acquired a certain honorific or decorative value.") Nervous lest she be considered nobody, the middle-class wife is careful to dress way up when she goes shopping. She knows by instinct what one middle-class woman told an inquiring sociologist: "You know there's class when you're in a department store and a well-dressed lady gets treated better."

"One who makes birth or wealth the sole criterion of worth": that's a conventional dictionary definition of a *snob*, and the place to look for the snob is in the middle class. Worried a lot about their own taste and about whether it's working for or against them, members of the middle class try to arrest their natural tendency to sink downward by associating themselves, if ever so tenuously, with the imagined possessors of money, power, and taste. "Correctness" and doing the right thing become obsessions, prompting middle-class people to write thank-you notes after the most ordinary dinner parties, give excessively expensive or correct

presents, and never allude to any place—Fort Smith,
Arkansas, for example—that lacks known class. It will
not surprise readers who have traveled extensively to
hear that Neil Mackwood, a British authority on snobbery, finds the greatest snobs worldwide emanating
from Belgium, which can also be considered world
headquarters of the middle class.

The desire to belong, and to belong by some mechanical act like purchasing something, is another sign
of the middle class. Words like *club* and *guild* (as in
Book-of-the-Month Club and Literary Guild) extend a
powerful invitation. The middle class is thus the natural
target for developers' ads like this:

> You Belong
>   in Park Forest!
> The moment you come to our town you know:
>   You're Welcome.
>   You're part of a big group. . . .

Oddity, introversion, and the love of privacy are the
big enemies, a total reversal of the values of the secure
upper orders. Among the middles there's a convention
that erecting a fence or even a tall hedge is an affront.
And there's also a convention that you may drop in
on neighbors or friends without a telephone inquiry
first. Being naturally innocent and well disposed and
aboveboard, a member of the middle class finds it hard
to believe that all are not. Being timid and conventional, no member of the middle class would expect
that anyone is copulating in the afternoon instead of
the evening, clearly, for busy and well-behaved corporate personnel, the correct time for it. When William
H. Whyte, Jr., was poking around one suburb studying
the residents, he was told by one quintessentially middle-class woman: "The street behind us is nowhere
near as friendly. They knock on doors over there."

If the women treasure "friendliness," the men treasure having a genteel occupation (usually more important than money), with emphasis on the word (if seldom the thing) *executive*. (As a matter of fact, an important class divide falls between those who feel veneration before the term *executive* and those who feel they want to throw up.) Having a telephone-answering machine at home is an easy way of simulating (at relatively low cost) high professional desirability, but here you wouldn't think of a facetious or eccentric text (delivered in French, for example, or in the voice of Donald Duck or Richard Nixon) asking the caller to speak his bit after the beeping sound. For the middle-class man is scared. As C. Wright Mills notes, "He is always somebody's man, the corporation's, the government's, the army's...." One can't be too careful.

PROLE COAT OF ARMS

One "management adviser" told Studs Terkel: "Your wife, your children have to behave properly. You've got to fit in the mold. You've got to be on guard." In *Coming Up for Air* (1939) George Orwell, speaking for his middle-class hero, gets it right:

> There's a lot of rot talked about the sufferings of the working class. I'm not so sorry for the proles myself.... The prole suffers physically, but he's a free man when he isn't working. But in every one of those little stucco boxes there's some poor bastard who's *never* free except when he's fast asleep.

Because he is essentially a salesman, the middle-class man develops a salesman's style. Hence his optimism and his belief in the likelihood of self-improvement if you'll just hurl yourself into it. One reason musicals like *Annie* and *Man of La Mancha* make so much money is that they offer him and his wife songs, like "Tomorrow" and "The Impossible Dream," that seem to promise that all sorts of good things are on their way. A final stigma of the middle class, an emanation of its social insecurity, is its habit of laughing at its own jests. Not entirely certain what social effect he's transmitting, and yet obliged, by his role as "salesman," to promote goodwill and optimism, your middle-class man serves as his own enraptured audience. Sometimes, after uttering some would-be clever formulation in public, he will look all around to gauge the response of the audience. Favorable, he desperately hopes.

The young men of the middle class are chips off the old block. If you want to know who reads John T. Molloy's books, hoping to break into the upper-middle class by formulas and mechanisms, they are your answer. You can see them on airplanes especially, being forwarded from one corporate training program to another. Their shirts are implausibly white, their suits are excessively dark, their neckties resemble those worn by undertakers, and their hair is cut in the style of the 1950s. Their talk is of *the bottom line*, and for *no* they are likely to say *no way*. Often their necks don't seem long enough, and their eyes tend to be too much in motion, flicking back and forth rather than up and down. They will enter adult life as corporate trainees and, after forty-five faithful years, leave it as corporate personnel, wondering whether this is all.

So much for the great middle class, to which, if you innocently credit people's descriptions of their own status, almost 80 percent of our population belongs. Proceeding downward, we would normally expect to meet next the lower-middle class. But it doesn't exist as such any longer, having been pauperized by the inflation of the 1960s and 1970s and transformed into the high-proletarian class. What's the difference? A further lack of freedom and self-respect. Our former lower-middle class, the new high proles, now head "the masses," and even if they are positioned at the top of the proletarian classes, still they are identifiable as people things are done to. They are in bondage—to monetary policy, rip-off advertising, crazes and delusions, mass low culture, fast foods, consumer schlock. Back in the 1940s there was still a real lower-middle class in this country, whose solid high-school education and addiction to "saving" and "planning" maintained it in a position—often precarious, to be sure—above the working class. In those days, says C. Wright Mills,

> there were fewer little men, and in their brief monopoly of high-school education they were in fact protected from many of the sharper edges of the workings of capitalist progress. They were free to

entertain deep illusions about their individual abil-
ities and about the collective trustworthiness of the
system. As their number has grown, however, they
have become increasingly subject to wage-worker
conditions.

Their social demotion has been the result. These
former low-white-collar people are now simply working machines, and the wife usually works as well as
the husband.

The kind of work performed and the sort of anxiety
that besets one as a result of work are ways to divide
the working class into its three strata. The high proles
are the skilled workers, craftsmen, like printers. The
mid-proles are the operators, like Ralph Kramden, the
bus driver. The low proles are unskilled labor, like
longshoremen. The special anxiety of the high proles
is fear about loss or reduction of status: you're proud
to be a master carpenter, and you want the world to
understand clearly the difference between you and a
laborer. The special anxiety of the mid-proles is fear
of losing the job. And of the low proles, the gnawing
perception that you're probably never going to make
enough or earn enough freedom to have and do the
things you want.

The kind of jobs high-prole people do tempt them
to insist that they are really "professionals," like "san-
itation men" in a large city. A mail carrier tells Studs
Terkel why he likes his work: "They always say, 'Here
comes the mailman.'...I feel it is one of the most
respected professions there is throughout the nation."
Prole women who go into nursing never tire of asserting
how professional they are, and the same is true of their
daughters who become air stewardesses, a favorite high-
prole occupation. Although Army officers, because they
are all terrified of the boss, are probably more middle-
class than high-prole, they seem the lower the more

they insist that they are "professionals," and since their disgrace in Vietnam, and their subsequent anxiety about their social standing, that insistence has grown more mechanical. An Army wife says, "Some like to speak of doctors, lawyers, etc., as professionals. All [Army] officers are professionals." And then, a notable deviation from logic: "Who could be more professional than the man who has dedicated his whole life to the defense of his country?"

One way to ascertain whether a person is middle-class or high-prole is to apply the principle that the wider the difference between one's working clothes and one's "best," the lower the class. Think not just of laborers and blue-collar people in general, but of doormen and bellboys, farmers and railway conductors and trainmen, and firemen. One of these once said: "I wish I was a lawyer. Shit, I wish I was a doctor. But I just didn't have it. You gotta have the smarts."

But high proles are quite smart, or at least shrewd. Because often their work is not closely supervised, they have pride and a conviction of independence, and they feel some contempt for those who have not made it as far as they have. They are, as the sociologist E. E. LeMasters calls them and titles his book, *Blue-Collar Aristocrats* (1975), and their disdain for the middle class is like the aristocrat's from the other direction. One high prole says: "If my boy wants to wear a goddamn necktie all his life and bow and scrape to some boss, that's his right, but by God he should also have the right to earn an honest living with his hands if that is what he likes." Like other aristocrats, says LeMasters, these "have gone to the top of their social world and need not expend time or energy on 'social climbing.'" They are aristocratic in other ways, like their devotion to gambling and their fondness for deer hunting. Indeed, the antlers with which they decorate their interiors give their dwellings in that respect a resemblance to the lodges of the Scottish peerage. The high prole resembles the aristocrat too, as Ortega y Gasset notes, in "his propensity to make out of games and sports the central occupation of his life," as well as in his unromantic attitude toward women.

Since they're not consumed with worry about choosing the correct status emblems, these people can be remarkably relaxed and unself-conscious. They can do, say, wear, and look like pretty much anything they want without undue feelings of shame, which belong to their betters, the middle class, shame being largely a bourgeois feeling. John Calvin, observes Jilly Cooper, is the prophet of the middle class, while Karl Marx is the prophet of the proles, even if most of them don't know it.

There are certain more or less infallible marks by which you can identify high proles. They're the ones who "belong" to Christmas and Channukah Clubs at banks, and they always buy big objects on installments. High proles are likely to spend money on things like elaborate color TVs, stereos, and tricky refrigerators, unlike the middles, who tend to invest in furniture of "good taste" to display in the living and dining room. Riding in sedans, high-prole men sit in front, with their wives planted in back. (As you move up to the middle class, one couple will be in front, one in back. But among upper-middles, you're likely to see a man and woman of different couples sharing a seat.) High proles arrive punctually at social events, social lateness of twenty minutes or so being a mark of the higher orders. If you're in a bar and you want to estimate the class of a man, get him, on some pretext, to take out his wallet. The high-prole wallet always bulges, not just with snaps of wife, children, and grandchildren to exhibit when the bearer grows maudlin, but with senti-

mental paper memorabilia like important sports-ticket
stubs and letters and other documents which can be
whipped out to "prove" things. The definitive high-
prole wallet has a wide rubber band around it.

All proles have a high respect for advertising and
brand names. By knowing about such things you can
display smartness and up-to-dateness, as well as associate yourself with the success of the products advertised. Drinking an identifiable bottle of Coca-Cola
outside on a hot day is not just drinking a Coke: it's
participating in a paradigm deemed desirable not just
by your betters—the Coca-Cola Company—but by
your neighbors, who perceive that you are doing something all-American and super-wonderful. John Brooks
has observed that the graffiti inscribers in the New
York subway cars tend to write everywhere but on the
advertising cards, "as if advertising were the one as-
pect of ... society that the writers can respect." Philip
Roth's Sophie Portnoy hovers between middle-class
and high-prole. If her habit of vigorous self-praise is
middle, her respect for advertised brand names and
her acute knowledge of prices is high-prole. "I'm the
only one who's good to her," she tells her son, referring
to the black cleaning woman. "I'm the only one who
gives her a whole can of tuna for lunch, and I'm not
talking dreck either, I'm talking Chicken of the Sea,
Alex ... 2 for 49!" *True Story*, aimed at "blue-collar
women," assures its advertisers, doubtless correctly,
that its readers are "the most brand-loyal group there
is." If you're a high prole you do the things a commercial society has decreed you're supposed to do. In
the Southwest, a place whose usages all of us are apparently expected to embrace in order to avoid "elitism," a popular high-prole family entertainment in the
evening is going out to the car wash, with a stop-in at

the local franchised food establishment on the way home. Or you might go to the Ice Show, titled, say, "Bugs Bunny in Space."

High proles are nice. It's down among the mid- and low proles that features some might find offensive begin to show themselves. These are the people who feel bitter about their work, often because they are closely supervised and regulated and generally treated like wayward children. "It's just like the Army," says an auto-assembly-plant worker. "No, it's worse.... You just about need a pass to piss." Andrews Levison, author of *The Working-Class Majority* (1974), invites us to imagine what it would be like to be under the constant eye of a foreman, "a figure who has absolutely no counterpart in middle-class society. Salaried professionals do often have people above them, but it is impossible to imagine professors or executives being required to bring a doctor's note if they are absent a day or having to justify the number of trips they take to the bathroom." Mid- and low proles are perceived to be so because they perform the role of the victims in that "coercive utilization of man by man" that Veblen found so objectionable. (Imposing the coercion, instead of having it imposed on you, is the prerogative of the more fortunate: managers, teachers, writers, journalists, clergy, film directors.)

The degree of supervision, indeed, is often a more eloquent class indicator than mere income, which suggests that the whole class system is more a recognition of the value of freedom than a proclamation of the value of sheer cash. The degree to which your work is overseen by a superior suggests your real class more accurately than the amount you take home from it. Thus the reason why a high-school teacher is "lower" than a tenured university professor. The teacher is obliged to file weekly "lesson plans" with a principal, superintendent, or "curriculum coordinator," thus acknowledging subservience. The professor, on the other hand, reports to no one, and his class is thus higher, even though the teacher may be smarter, better-mannered, and richer. (It is in public schools, the postal service, and police departments that we meet terms like *supervisor* and *inspector*: the prole hunter will need to know no more.) One is a mid- or low prole if one's servitude is constantly emphasized. Occupational class depends very largely on doing work for which the consequences of error or failure are distant or remote, or better, invisible, rather than immediately apparent to a superior and thus instantly humiliating to the performer.

Constantly demeaned at work, the lower sorts of proles suffer from poor morale. As one woman worker says, "Most of us . . . have jobs that are too small for our spirit." A taxi driver in St. Louis defended the Vietnam War by saying, "We can't be a pitiful, helpless giant. We gotta show 'em we're number one." "Are you number one?" Studs Terkel asked him. Pause. "I'm number nothin'," he said. There's a prole tendency to express class disappointment by self-simplification, and when examining proles it's well to be mindful of the observation of British critic Richard Hoggart: "There are no simple people. The 'ordinary' is complex too." Robert Bly would agree, as his poem "Come with Me" suggests:

> Come with me into those things that have felt this
> despair for so long—
> Those removed Chevrolet wheels that howl with a
> terrible loneliness,
> Lying on their backs in the cindery dirt, like men
> drunk, and naked,
> Staggering off down a hill at night to drown at last
> in the pond.

Those shredded inner tubes abandoned on the
    shoulders of thruways,
Black and collapsed bodies, that tried and burst,
And were left behind;
And the curly steel shavings, scattered about on
    garage benches,
Sometimes still warm, gritty when we hold them,
Who have given up, and blame everything on the
    government,
And those roads in South Dakota that feel around
    in the darkness . . .

"A click": that's who runs things, say mid- and low
proles, retreating into their private pursuits: home
workshops and household repairs, washing and polishing the car; playing poker; fishing, hunting, camp-
ing; watching sports and Westerns on TV and
identifying with quarterback or hero; visiting relatives
(most upper-middles and uppers, by contrast, are in
flight from their relatives and visit friends instead);
family shopping at the local mall on Saturday or Sunday.

At the bottom of the working class, the low prole
is identifiable by the gross uncertainty of his employment. This class would include illegal aliens like Mexican fruit pickers as well as other migrant workers.
Social isolation is the norm here, and what Hoggart
says of the lower working class in Britain applies elsewhere as well: "Socially . . . each day and each week
is almost unplanned. There is no diary, no book of
engagements, and few letters are sent or received."
Remoteness and isolation, as in the valleys of Appa-
lachia, are characteristics, and down here we find people who, trained for nothing, are likely out of sheer
wayward despair to join the Army.

Still, they're better off than the destitute, who never
have even seasonal work and who live wholly on welfare. They differ from the bottom-out-of-sights less be-

cause they're much better off than because they're
more visible, in the form of Bowery bums, bag ladies,
people who stand in public places lecturing and deliv-
ering harangues about their grievances, people who
drink out of paper bags, people whose need for some
recognition impels them to "act" in front of audiences
in the street. When delinquency and distress grow desperate, you sink into the bottom-out-of-sight class,
staying all day in your welfare room or contriving to
get taken into an institution, whether charitable or correctional doesn't matter much.

Thus the classes. They are usefully imagined as a
line of theaters running side by side down a long street.
Each has a marquee and lots of posters on the front.
Plays about self-respect are running constantly in all
of them, from the most comfortable to the barest and
meanest. But the odd thing is that there's no promotion
from one theater to the next one up. And the important
point is this: there's no one playing in any of these
theaters, no matter how imposing, who isn't, much of
the time, scared to death that he's going to stumble,
muff his lines, appear in the wrong costume, or otherwise bomb. If you find an American who feels entirely class-secure, stuff and exhibit him. He's a rare
specimen.

❡[III]❡

APPEARANCE COUNTS

How IS IT THAT IF YOU'RE SHARP, YOU'RE GENERALLY able to estimate a person's class at a glance? What caste marks do you look for?

Good looks, first of all, distributed around the classes pretty freely, to be sure, but frequently a mark of high caste. Prudent natural selection is the reason, as Jilly Cooper perceives. She notes that if upper-class people marry downward, they tend to choose beauty only, and concludes: "In general, good-looking people marry up . . . and the insecure and ugly tend to marry down." Smiling is a class indicator—that is, not doing a lot of it. On the street, you'll notice that prole women smile more, and smile wider, than those of the middle and upper classes. They like showing off their pretty dentures, for one thing, and for another, they're enmeshed in the "have a nice day" culture and are busy effusing a defensive optimism much of the time. And speaking of dentures, I witnessed recently an amazing performance in which a prole man in a public place dropped his top plate into a position where he could thrust it forward with his tongue until, pink and yellow, it protruded an inch or so from his mouth. The intent seemed

47

to be to "air" it. Now one simply can't imagine the middle or upper-middle classes doing that sort of thing, although you'd not be surprised to see an upper-class person, utterly careless of public opinion as he'd be, doing it.

Sheer height is a more trustworthy sign of class in England than everywhere, but classy people are seldom short and squat, even here. Regardless of one's height, having an ass that protrudes is low, as is having, or appearing to have, very little neck. The absence of neck is notable in Lawrence Welk, country-and-Western singers like Johnny Cash, and similar proles. If you're skeptical that looks give off class messages, in your imagination try conflating Roy Acuff with Averell Harriman, or Mayor Daley with George Bush. Or, for that matter, Minnie Pearl with Jackie Onassis.

Because 62 percent of Americans are overweight, a cheap way to achieve a sort of distinction is to be thin. This is the general aim of the top four classes, although the middle, because its work tends to be sedentary, has a terrible time abstaining from the potatoes. Destitutes and bottom-out-of-sights usually don't go around flaunting a lot of extra flesh, but seldom from choice. It's the three prole classes that get fat: fast foods and beer are two of the causes, but anxiety about slipping down a rung, resulting in nervous overeating, plays its part too, especially among high proles. Proles can rationalize their fat as an announcement of steady wages and the ability to eat out often: even "Going Out for Breakfast" is a thinkable operation for proles, if we believe they respond to the McDonald's TV ads the way they're conditioned to.

A recent magazine ad for a diet book aimed at proles stigmatizes a number of erroneous assumptions about weight, proclaiming with some inelegance that "They're All a Crock." Among vulgar errors thus rejected is the

"YOUR WEIGHT IS AN ADVERTISEMENT OF YOUR SOCIAL
STANDING."

proposition that "All Social Classes Are Equally Overweight." The ad explains:

> Your weight is an advertisement of your social
> standing. A century ago, corpulence was a sign of
> success. But no more. Today it is the badge of the
> lower-middle class, where obesity is *four times* more
> prevalent than it is among the upper-middle and
> middle classes.

And not just four times more prevalent. Four times
more visible, for flaunting obesity is a prole sign, as if
the object were to offer maximum aesthetic offense to
the higher classes and thus exact a form of revenge.
Jonathan Raban, watching people at the Minnesota

State Fair, was vouchsafed a spectacle suggesting calculated, vigorously intentional obesity:

> These farming families... were the descendants of hungry immigrants from Germany and Scandinavia.... Generation by generation, their families had eaten themselves into Americans. Now they all had the same figure: same broad bottom, same buddha belly, same neckless join between turkey-wattle chin and sperm-whale torso. The women had poured themselves into pink elasticized pantsuits; the men swelled against every seam and button of their plaid shirts and Dacron slacks.

And lest they not be sufficiently noticed, Raban reports, many of the men wore caps asking us to believe that, in opposition to the wisdom of the ages, "Happiness Is Being a Grandparent." Raban found himself so fascinated by U.S.A. fat that he proposes a Fatness Map, which would indicate that the fattest people live in areas where the immigration has been the most recent and "ancestral memories of hunger closest." On the other hand, "states... settled before 1776 would register least in the way of fatty tissue. Girth would generally increase from east to west and from south to north. The flab capital of the U.S.A. should be located somewhere in the triangle of Minnesota, Iowa, and the Dakotas."

We don't have to go all the way with Raban to preceive that there is an elite look in this country. It requires women to be thin, with a hairstyle dating back eighteen or twenty years or so. (The classiest women wear their hair for a lifetime in exactly the style they affected in college.) They wear superbly fitting dresses and expensive but always understated shoes and handbags, with very little jewelry. They wear scarves— these instantly betoken class, because they are useless except as a caste mark. Men should be thin. No jewelry at all. No cigarette case. Moderate-length hair, never dyed or tinted, which is a middle-class or high-prole sign, as the practice of President Reagan indicates. Never a hairpiece, a prole usage. (High and mid-proles call them *rugs*, *mats*, or *doilies*. Calling them *toops* is low-prole.) Both women's and men's elite looks are achieved by a process of rejection—of the current, the showy, the superfluous. Thus the rejection of fat by the elite. Michael Korda in his book *Success!* gets the point. "It pays," he finds, "to be thin."

But the elite rejection of the superfluous in no way implies a "minimal" look in clothes. Rather, "layering" is obligatory. As Alison Lurie says in *The Language of Clothes* (1981), "It has generally been true that the more clothes someone has on, the higher his or her status." And she goes on: "The recent fashion for 'layered' clothes may be related, as is sometimes claimed, to the energy shortage; it is also a fine way of displaying a large wardrobe."

The upper-middle-class woman will appear almost invariably in a skirt of gray flannel, Stuart plaid, or khaki; a navy-blue cardigan, which may be cable-stitched; a white blouse with Peter Pan collar; hose with flat shoes; hair preferably in a barrette. When it gets cold, she puts on a blue blazer, or, for business, a gray flannel suit. But the color toward which everything aspires is really navy. There will be lots of layering and a tendency to understate. The indispensable accessory will be a glasses case decorated with home-made needlepoint (an important caste mark: the needlepoint suggests hours of aimless leisure during which someone has worked on it—unthinkable for proles). If a woman does a lot of knitting for family and friends, chances are she's upper-middle-class. But if when she finishes a sweater she sews in a little label reading

Handmade by Gertrude Willis

she's middle-class. If the label reads

Hand-crafted by Gertrude Willis

she's high-prole.

If navy is the upper-middle-class color, purple is the prole equivalent, and it is scourged frequently by Barbara Blaes, wardrobe adviser to the Departments of Labor and Commerce as well as the CIA and the Food and Drug Administration. She gets $400 a day for rooting out prole garments from among women working in government departments. What she wants women to look like, as much as possible, is female men, in navy or gray tailored suits. Not, most assuredly, the pantsuit, especially not in purple, and especially not in purple polyester. That is the absolute bottom, the classic prole costume. It's right down there with another favorite prole getup, this one favored by the slender the way the pantsuit is by the obese. I refer to designer jeans worn with very high heels. This is a common outfit among newcomers to the suburbs who've not yet mastered the pseudo-prep, upper-middle look.

The purple polyester pantsuit offends two principles that determine class in clothes: the color principle and the organic-materials principle. Navy blue aside, colors are classier the more pastel or faded, and materials are classier the more they consist of anything that was once alive. That means wool, leather, silk, cotton, and fur. Only. All synthetic fibers are prole, partly because they're cheaper than natural ones, partly because they're not archaic, and partly because they're entirely uniform and hence boring—you'll never find a bit of straw or sheep excrement woven into an acrylic sweater. Veblen got the point in 1899, speaking of mass-produced goods in general: "Machine-made goods of daily use are often admired and preferred precisely on account of their excessive perfection by the vulgar and the underbred, who have not given due thought to the punctilios of elegant consumption." (The organic principle also determines that in kitchens wood is classier than Formica, and on the kitchen table a cotton cloth "higher" than plastic or oilcloth.) So important for genuine upper-middle-class standing is the total renunciation of artificial fibers that the elite eye becomes skilled in detecting even, as *The Official Preppy Handbook* has it, "a small percentage of polyester in an Oxford-cloth shirt"—a sad middle-caste mark. The same invaluable book praises young Caroline Kennedy unreservedly—"on technical points Preppier than Mummy"—because "during four years at Harvard Square, an unnatural fiber never went near her body." It somehow seems very American and very late-twentieth-century—that is, very prole—that we are now invited to buy bath towels, whose only office is to absorb moisture, with their cotton, the sole absorbing fiber they contain, carefully diluted by 12 percent Dacron polyester to keep them from absorbing so well.

But no one talks that way without risking rebuke from Mr. Fisher A. Rhymes, Director of Public Affairs of the Man-Made Fiber Producers Association, with headquarters in Washington, where it's in a position to persuade the Army and Navy to introduce the maximum number of man-made fibers not just into their towels but into their mops and sponges as well. Mr. Rhymes stands ready at all times to rebut calumnies, as he does in a recent letter to the *New York Times* defending polyester against a fashion writer's strictures. "Polyester," he says, "in its many luxurious forms, is the most widely used fashion fiber today." (Just what's wrong with it, of course, from the class point of view.)

If you can gauge people's proximity to prole status

by the color and polyester content of their garments,
legibility of their dress is another sign. "Legible clothing" is Alison Lurie's useful term to designate things
like T-shirts or caps with messages on them you're
supposed to read and admire. The messages may be
simple, like BUDWEISER or HEINEKEN's, or they may
be complex and often lewd, like the one on the girl's
T-shirt: THE BEST PART IS INSIDE. When proles assem-
ble to enjoy leisure, they seldom appear in clothing
without words on it. As you move up the classes and
the understatement principle begins to operate, the
words gradually disappear, to be replaced, in the middle and upper-middle classes, by mere emblems, like
the Lacoste alligator. Once, ascending further, you've
left all such trademarks behind, you may correctly infer
that you are entering the purlieus of the upper class
itself. The same reason a T-shirt reading COKE'S THE
REAL THING is prole determines that the necktie reading COUNTESS MARA is vulgar and middle-class.

LEGIBLE CLOTHING, MIDDLE CLASS (LEFT) AND PROLE

There are psychological reasons why proles feel a need to wear legible clothing, and they are more touching than ridiculous. By wearing a garment reading SPORTS ILLUSTRATED or GATORADE or LESTER LANIN, the prole associates himself with an enterprise the world judges successful, and thus, for the moment, he achieves some importance. This is the reason why, at the Indianapolis Motor Speedway each May, you can see grown men walking around proud to wear silly-looking caps so long as they say GOODYEAR or VAL-VOLINE. Brand names today possess a totemistic power to confer distinction on those who wear them. By donning legible clothing you fuse your private identity with external commercial success, redeeming your insignificance and becoming, for the moment, somebody. For $27 you can send in to a post-office box in Holiday, Florida, and get a nylon jacket in blue, white, and orange that says, on the front, UNION 76. There are sizes for kids and ladies too. Just the thing for the picnic. And this need is not the proles' alone. Witness the T-shirts and carryalls stamped with the logo of *The New York Review of Books*, which convey the point "I read hard books," or printed with portraits of Mozart and Haydn and Beethoven, which assure the world, "I am civilized." The gold-plated blazer buttons displaying university seals affected by the middle class likewise identify the wearer with impressive brand names like the University of Indiana and Louisiana State.

The wearing of clothes either excessively new or excessively neat and clean also suggests that your social circumstances are not entirely secure. The upper and upper-middle classes like to appear in old clothes, as if to advertise how much of conventional dignity they can afford to throw away, as the men of these classes do also when they abjure socks while wearing loafers. Douglas Sutherland, in *The English Gentleman* (1980), is sound on the old-clothes principle. "Gentlemen," he writes, "may wear their suits until they are threadbare but they do so with considerable panache and it is evident to the most uncritical eye that they have been built by a good tailor." On the other hand, the middle class and the proles make much of new clothes, of course with the highest possible polyester content. The question of the class meaning of cleanliness is a tricky one, not as easy, perhaps, as Alison Lurie thinks. She finds cleanliness "a sign of status, since to be clean and neat always involves the expense of time and money." But laboring to present yourself scrupulously clean and neat suggests that you're worried about status slippage and that you care terribly what your audience thinks, both low signs. The perfect shirt collar, the too neatly tied necktie knot, the anxious overattention to dry cleaning—all betray the wimp. Or the nasty-nice. The deployment of the male bowtie is an illustration. If neatly tied, centered, and balanced, the effect is middle-class. When tied askew, as if carelessly or incompetently, the effect is upper-middle or even, if sufficiently inept, upper. The worst thing is being neat when, socially, you're supposed to be sloppy, or clean when you're supposed to be filthy. There's an analogy here with the excessively washed and polished automobile, almost infallibly a sign of prole ownership. Class people can afford to drive dirty cars. Just as, walking on the street, they're more likely to carry their business papers in tatty expanding files made of reddish-brown fiber, now fuzzy and sweat-stained, rather than in neat-looking attaché cases displaying lots of leather and brass, items that are a sad stigma of the middle class.

This principle of not-too-neat is crucial in men's clothing. Too careful means low—at least middle-class, perhaps prole. "Dear boy, you're almost too well dressed to be a gentleman," Neil Mackwood, author of *Debrett's In and Out* (1980), imagines an upper-class person addressing someone in the middle class, as if the speaker were implying that the addressee is not a gent but a model, a floorwalker, or an actor. "A now famous Hollywood actor," Vance Packard reports, "still reveals his lower...origins every time he sits down. He pulls up his trousers to preserve the crease." And King George IV is said to have observed of Robert Peel: "He's not a gentleman: he divides his coattails when he sits down."

The difference between high- versus low-caste effects in men's clothes is partly the result of the upper orders' being used to wearing suits, or at least jackets. As Lurie perceives, the suit "not only flatters the inactive, it deforms the laborious." (And the athletic or strenuously muscular: Arnold Schwartzenegger looks especially comic in a suit.) For this reason the suit— preferably the "dark suit"—was a prime weapon in the nineteenth-century war of the bourgeoisie against the proletariat. "The triumph of the...suit," says Lurie, "meant that the blue-collar man in his best clothes was at his worst in any formal confrontation with his 'betters.'" We can think of blacksmith Joe Gargary in Dickens's *Great Expectations*, dressed miserably to the nines for an appearance in the city, being patronized by the comfortably dressed Pip.

"This strategic disadvantage," Lurie goes on, "can still be seen in operation at local union-management confrontations, in the offices of banks and loan companies, and whenever a working-class man visits a government bureau." That's an illustration of John T. Molloy's general principle of the way men use clothing to convey class signals. When two men meet, he perceives, "One man's clothing is saying to the other man,

'I am more important than you are, please show respect'; or, 'I am your equal and expect to be treated as such'; or, 'I am not your equal and do not expect to be treated as such.'" For this reason, Molloy indicates, proles who want to rise must be extremely careful to affect "Northeastern establishment attire," which will mean that Brooks Brothers and J. Press will be their guides: "Business suits should be plain; no fancy or extra buttons; no weird color stitching; no flaps on the breast pocket; no patches on the sleeves; no belts in the back of the jacket; no leather ornamentation; no cowboy yokes. Never."

It's largely a matter of habit and practice, says C. Wright Mills in *The Power Elite* (1956): no matter where you live, he insists, "anyone with the money and the inclination can learn to be uncomfortable in anything but a Brooks Brothers suit." And, I would add, can learn to recoil from clothes with a glossy (middle-class) as opposed to a matte (upper-middle-class) finish. Middle-class clothes tend to err by excessive smoothness, to glitter a bit, to shine even before they're worn. Upper-middle clothes, on the other hand, lean to the soft, textured, woolly, nubby. Ultimately, the difference implies a difference between *city* and *country*, or labor and leisure, where *country* betokens not decrepit dairy farms and bad schools but estates and horse-leisure. Thus the popularity among the upper-middle class (and the would-be upper-middle class, like members of Ivy university faculties) of the tweed jacket. Country leisure is what it implies, not daily wage slavery in the city.

The tweed jacket is indispensable to the upper-middle-class trick of layering. A man signals that he's classy if, outdoors, he comes on in a tweed jacket, with vest or sweater (or two), shirt, tie, long wool scarf, and overcoat or raincoat. An analogy is with the upper-class house, which has lots of different rooms for dif-

ferent purposes. Wearing one shirt over another—
Oxford-cloth button-down over a turtleneck, for example—is upper-middle-class, and the shirt worn underneath can even be a dress shirt (solid color is best)
with its own collar, a usage I've seen in warm weather
on Madison Avenue in the upper eighties. Since sweaters are practically obligatory for layering, it's important to know that the classiest is the Shetland crew-
neck pullover, and in "Scottish" colors—heather and
the like, especially when a tieless Oxford-cloth shirt
(palpably without artificial fibers) just peeps over the
top. Add a costly tweed jacket without shoulder padding and no one can tell you're not upper-middle at
least. The V-neck sweater, designed to prove conclu-
sively that you're wearing a necktie, is for that reason
middle-class or even high prole. It's hard to believe
that sometimes people tuck pullovers into the top of
their trousers, but I'm told they do. If this does happen,
it's a very low sign.

The interpreter of men's class appearances can
hardly do better than study the costumes of the Presidents as they come and go. The general principle here
is that the two-button suit is more prole than the three-
button Eastern-establishment model. Most Presidents
have worn the two-button kind before, and when they
assume the leadership of the Free World, they feel
obliged to change, now affecting three-button suits and
resembling the Chairman of the Board of the Chase
Manhattan Bank. This is what made Richard Nixon
look so awkward most of the time. He was really comfortable in the sort of Klassy Kut two-button suit you
might wear if you were head of the Savings & Loan
Association of Whittier, California. His successor,
Gerald Ford, although brought up on the hick two-
button model, managed to wear the three-button job
with some plausibility, being more pliable and perhaps
a faster study than Nixon. But he never really pulled

off the con, in features resembling as he did Joe Pa-
looka rather than any known type of American aristocrat. James Earl Carter knew himself well enough
to realize that he should reject two- and three-button
suits alike, sticking to blue jeans and thus escaping
criticism as one who aspires to the Establishment but
fails.

Ronald Reagan, of course, doesn't need to affect
the establishment style, sensing accurately that his
lowbrow, God-fearing, intellect-distrusting constitu-
ency regards it as an affront (which, of course, to them
it is). Reagan's style can be designated Los Angeles
(or even Orange) County Wasp-Chutzpah. It registers
the sense that if you stubbornly believe you're as good
as educated and civilized people—i.e., those Eastern
dudes—then you are. He is the perfect representative
of the mind and soul of the Sun Belt. He favors, of
course, the two-button suit with maximum shoulder
padding and with a Trumanesque squared white handkerchief in the breast pocket, which makes him look,
when he's dressed way up, like a prole setting off for
church. Sometimes, for leisure activities (as he might
express it), he affects the cowboy look, which, especially when one is aged, appeals mightily to the Sun
Belt seniles. One hesitates even to speculate about the
polyester levels of his outfits.

Indeed, Reagan violates virtually every canon of
upper-class or even upper-middle-class presentation.
The dyed hair is, as we've seen, an outrage, as is the
rouge on the cheeks. (Will the President soon proceed
to eye shadow and liner?) So is the white broadcloth
shirt with its omnipresent hint of collar stays. (Anxiety
about neatness.) The suit materials are scandalously
bucolic middle-class: plaid, but never Glen plaid. The
necktie is tied with a full Windsor knot, the favorite
of sophisticated high-school boys everywhere. When

after a press conference Dan Rather, not everyone's idea of a Preppy, comes on to "summarize" and try to make sense of the President's vagaries, his light-blue Oxford-cloth button-down and "regimental" tie make him, by contrast, look upper-middle-class. The acute student of men's class signals could virtually infer Reagan's politics of Midwestern small-town meanness from his getups, just as one might deduce Roosevelt's politics of aristocratic magnanimity from such classy accessories as his naval cape, pince-nez, and cigarette holder.

It's not just Ronald Reagan who violates all canons of gentlemanly attire. It's the conspicuous members of his "team" as well, like Al Haig. (Even though he's no longer Secretary of State, he wants so much to be President that he's appropriately dealt with here.) It's cruel, of course, to demand that a soldier know anything about taste on those occasions when he's obliged to disguise himself as an ordinary person. (Although there's always the example of General George C. Marshall, who, after a lifetime of appearing in uniform, managed in mufti to wear the three-button, three-piece suit as if to the classy manner born.) Al Haig's class stigma is the gaping jacket collar, always a prole giveaway. Here, the collar of the jacket separates itself from the collar of the shirt and backs off and up an inch or so: the effect is that of a man coming apart. That this caste mark is without specifically reactionary political meaning is confirmed by a photograph of Richard Hoggart, the British radical critic and Labour Party enthusiast, used to promote a recent book of his: his jacket collar is gaping a full inch at the rear, ample indication that jacket gape afflicts the far left as well as the far right. What it betrays, indeed, is less the zealot than the stooge. Like the poor chap interviewed on TV recently by William F. Buckley. He was from

Texas and wanted to censor school textbooks to repress, among other evils, *pro-mís-kitty*. (As gently as
possible, Buckley corrected this mispronunciation of
promiscuity so that the audience would know what the
poor ass was talking about.) But even if the Texan had
not, with complete confidence in his unaided powers,
delivered repeatedly this prole mispronunciation, his
perceptiveness and sensibility could have been inferred
from the way his jacket collar gaped open *a full two
inches*. Buckley's collar, of course, clung tightly to his
neck and shoulders, turn and bow and bob as he might.
And here I will reject all accusations that I am favoring
the rich over the poor. The distinction I'm pointing to
is not one between the tailored clothes of the fortunate
and the store clothes of the others, for if you try you
can get a perfectly fitting suit collar off the rack, or at
least have it altered to fit snugly. The difference is in
recognizing this as a class signal and not being aware
of it as such. You've got to know that, as Douglas
Sutherland says in *The English Gentleman*, almost the
most important criterion in a suit worth wearing at all
is "that it should fit well round the shoulders."

In addition to the gaping "Haig" or "stooge" jacket
collar, there are two other low signals, visible usually
when the subject is unjacketed, which instantly proclaim the wearer either middle-class or high-prole. They
are, first, the nerd pack, and second, belt hangdowns
of any kind. The nerd pack is that little plastic enve-
lope, often with advertising on the outer flap, worn in
the breast pocket of a shirt to prevent pens and pencils
from soiling the acrylic. In the nerd-pack trade, it is
called a "Pocket Protector." One mail-order catalog
aimed at high proles assures you that your nerd pack
can be personalized with a three-letter monogram. Nerd
packs are favored by people obliged to simulate efficiency, like supermarket managers, or by people hop-

PROLE JACKET-GAPE

ing to give the impression that their need to pull out a pen is virtually constant, like itinerant insurance salesmen.

Belt hangdowns, usually of real or fake leather, are another all but infallible signal of middle-classness or even outright prolehood. These vary from slide-rule cases, at the top, all the way down to dark-glasses cases, cigarette-pack holders "with Western hand-tooling," and—in a catalog—an "Eyeglass and Pen Holster: Deluxe Cowhide, Personalized with Your Initials." The term *holster* suggests the would-be macho implications of all these belt attachments. The fact that these hangdowns are usually high-prole indicates the social class of the low homosexuals who advertise their "sexual preferences" by wearing key rings on their belts, dangling from left or right, front or rear, as the case may be. One reason we may feel it difficult for an engineer ever to be upper-middle-class is that even in college he's begun this habitual daily wearing of belt hangdowns—if not slide rules or calculators, then low tools like geology picks and the like.

Imagine a man dressed in the summer costume appropriate for his work. He's wearing a short-sleeved white shirt (Dacron, largely), a necktie, dark trousers, and a nerd pack. He's a middle-class or high-prole clerk in a hardware store. Now notice: all you have to do to turn him into an "engineer" is to add one or more belt hangdowns and pop a white hardhat onto his head. Thus the social-class problems of engineers, uncertain always where they fit, whether with boss or worker, management or labor, the world of headwork or the world of handwork. And actually, anything attached to the belt, even if it doesn't ignominiously hang down, is a high-prole sign. Sunglasses, for example, in an artificial leather case. Rather than sport them on your belt, it's better even to let them dangle by the sidepiece from the top buttonhole of your shirt—a middle-class but at least not a prole habit.

If nerd packs and belt hangdowns instantly imply prole leanings, there are other signs almost as clear. When you're wearing a shirt with a sweater or jacket over it but omitting a necktie, what do you do with the shirt collar? Keeping all of it inside both sweater and jacket is upper- or upper-middle-class, partly, I suppose, because the effect is "careless" rather than "neat." On the other hand, displaying it spread out over the jacket collar, unless you're a member of the Israeli Knesset or teach at the Hebrew University, is flagrantly middle-class or prole—and may be even then. All you really have to know about this practice is that when out riding or otherwise got up in sports costume, the President favors it.

Shirts, indeed, are among the most class-eloquent garments, and there are countless ways you can lose caste through their agency. Wearing "white on white" is an easy way to drop to middle or high prole, while wearing a vest over a short-sleeved shirt or—like Ed Norton, in *The Honeymooners*—over a T-shirt will sink you to mid- or low prole. Sometimes one sees suspenders worn over a T-shirt, the equivalent of socks worn with sandals. In England especially, but also in Anglophile parts of the United States, these usages suggest that you're a middle-class secondary-school teacher of math or chemistry who, by appearing in his holiday garb, is secretly lusting for demotion to high prole.

Jewelry is another instant class-lowerer, like the enameled little Old Glory lapel pins worn by the insane and by cynical politicians working backward districts. When their ladies wear them with the colors picked out in rhinestones, the effect is even lower—deep-prole, shall we say. The general class rule about wrist-watches is, the more "scientific," technological, and space-age, the lower. Likewise with the more "information" the watch is supposed to convey, like the time of day in Kuala Lumpur, the number of days elapsed in the year so far, or the current sign of the zodiac. Some upper-class devotees of the Cartier tank watch with the black lizard strap will argue that even a second hand compromises a watch's class, implying as it may the wearer's need for great accuracy, as if he were something like a professional timer of bus arrivals and departures. The other upper-class watch is the cheapest and simplest Timex, worn with a grosgrain-ribbon strap, changed often: black ones for formal wear are amusing. One prole mistake is to conceive cuff links classy, especially ones like those in the wardrobe of Kurt Vonnegut's Billy Pilgrim, the optometrist hero of *Slaughterhouse-Five*: simulated Roman coins, quite large; little roulette wheels that actually turn; and "another pair which had a real thermometer in one and a real compass in the other." These come close to the cuff links made of the "finest specimens of human molars" which Meyer Wolfsheim in *The Great Gatsby* is proud to call attention to.

Another significant social-class divide is the color of the raincoat. After extensive and really quite impressive research, John T. Molloy has discovered that in raincoat colors beige far outranks black, olive, or dark blue. The black raincoat proves to be, indeed, a highly trustworthy prole sign. Thus Molloy exhorts his prole readers ambitious to acquire an upper-middle-class look to equip themselves with beige raincoats as soon as possible. The implication of beige, one supposes, is that it advertises one's greater carelessness about the risk of stains: there's a go-to-hell air about it that doesn't attend the prudent black number. You will not be at all surprised now to hear that in *I Love Lucy* the raincoat worn by Ricky Ricardo is black.

Go-to-hell in spirit also are the sports or playtime trousers which identify the upper-middle class, especially the suburban branch. One common type is white duck trousers with little green frogs embroidered all over them. A variation: light-green trousers, with dark-blue embroidered whales. Or signal flags. Or bell buoys. buoys. Or lobsters. Or anything genteel-marine, suggesting that the wearer has just strolled a few steps away from his good-sized yacht. Thus also the class usefulness of Topsider shoes, the ones with the white soles "for gripping wet decks." The same with windbreakers displaying lots of drawstrings. The Chris-Craft mail-order catalog will show you the look to imitate, but classes much below the upper middle should take warning that they're unlikely to affect this yachtsman's look with much plausibility. A lot depends on a certain habitual carelessness in the carriage, a quasi-wind-blown calculated sloppiness. It's almost impossible to imitate, and you should have a long thin neck, too.

The topic of the class implications of men's neckties deserves a book in itself. Here I can only sketch a few general principles. Skimpy as its contribution of fabric to the total ensemble may be, the tie does add to the effect of layering and for this reason if for no other is identified with high status. But it must be said too that in the right context omitting the tie entirely conveys the message that one is so classy—say, upper-class—as to be above all criticism, and that conventional canons of respectability don't apply. The necktie's association with responsibility, good employeeship, and other presumed attributes of the obedient middle class is well documented by an experiment conducted by Molloy. He had a series of men interviewed for good jobs. Some wore ties, others did not. "Invariably," he found,

> those men who wore their ties to interviews were offered jobs; those without them were turned down. And in one almost incredible situation, the interviewer...was made so uncomfortable by the applicant's lack of a tie that he gave the man $6.50, told him to go out and buy a tie, put it on, and then come back to complete the interview. He still didn't get the job.

The same suggestion that the necktie is an important marker of the division between the middle and the prole classes emerges from another of Molloy's experiments, this one performed at the horrible Port Authority Bus Terminal in New York, a traditional locus of every imaginable vice, menace, and outrage. He himself posed as a middle-class man who had left his wallet home and had somehow to get back to the suburbs. At the rush hour, he tried to borrow 75 cents for his bus fare, the first hour wearing a suit but no tie, the second hour properly dressed, tie and all. "In the first hour," he reports, "I made $7.23, but in the second, with my tie on, I made $26, and one man even gave me extra money for a newspaper."

The principle that clothing moves lower in status the more legible it becomes applies to neckties with a vengeance. The ties worn by the top classes eschew the more obvious forms of verbal or even too crudely symbolic statement, relying on stripes, amoeba-like foulard blobs, or small dots to make the point that the wearer possesses too much class to care to specify right out in front what it's based on. (This illustrates the privacy principle, or the principle of mind-your-own-little-disgusting-middle-class-business, a customary element of the aristocratic stance.) Small white dots against a dark background, perhaps the most conservative tie possible, are favored both by uppers and upper-middles and, defensively, by those nervous about being thought low, coarse, drunken, or cynical, like journalists and TV news readers and sportscasters, and by those whose fiduciary honor must be thought beyond question, like the trust officers working for the better metropolitan banks.

Moving down from stripes, blobs, or dots, we come to necktie patterns with a more overt and precise semiotic function. Some, designed to announce that the upper-middle-class wearer is a sport, will display diagonal patterns of little flying pheasants, or small yachts, signal flags, and sextants. ("I hunt and own a yacht. Me rich and sporty!") Just below these are the "milieu" patterns, designed to celebrate the profession of the wearer and to congratulate him on having so fine a profession. These are worn either by insecure members of the upper-middle-class (like surgeons) or by members of the middle class aspiring to upper-middle status (like accountants). Thus a tie covered with tiny caduceuses proclaims "Hot damn! I am a physician." (Significantly, there is no milieu tie pattern for dentists.) Little scales signify "I am a lawyer." Musical notes: "I have something to do with music." Dollar signs, or money bags: a stockbroker, banker, perhaps a wildly successful plastic surgeon, or a lottery winner. I've even seen one tie with a pattern of little jeeps, whose meaning I've found baffling, for surely if you were a *driver* in any of our wars you'd not be likely to announce it. Other self-congratulatory patterns like little whales or dolphins or seals can suggest that you love nature and spend a lot of time protecting it and are thus a fine person. Any of these milieu ties can be alternated with the "silk rep" model striped with the presumed colors of British (never, *never* German, French, Italian, Spanish, Portuguese, or White Russian) regiments, clubs, or universities.

As we move further down the class hierarchy, actual words begin to appear on ties, and these are meant to be commented on by viewers. One such exhibitionist artifact is the Grandfather's Tie in dark blue with grandchildren's names hand-painted on it, diagonally, in white. Imagine the conversations that ensue when you wear it! Another kind reads "I'd rather be sailing," "skiing," etc., and these can also be effective underminers of privacy—"conversation-starters," and thus useful adjuncts to comfy middle-class status, in the tradition of expecting neighbors to drop in without warning. Some ties down in this stratum affect great cleverness, reading "Thank God It's Friday" or "Oh Hell, It's Monday"; and a way to get a chuckle out of your audience and at the same time raise your class a bit is to have these sentiments abbreviated on your tie with yachting signal flags. At the bottom of the middle class, just before it turns to high prole, we encounter ties depicting large flowers in brilliant colors, or simply bright "artistic" splotches. The message is frequently "I'm a merry dog." These wearers are the ones Molloy is addressing when, discussing neckties, he warns, "Avoid purple under all circumstances."

Further down still, where questions of yacht ownership or merry doghood are too preposterous to be claimed even on a necktie, we come upon the high- or mid-prole "bola" tie, a woven or leather thong with a slide (often of turquoise or silver), affected largely by retired persons residing in Sun Belt places like New Mexico. Like any other sort of tie, this one makes a statement, saying: "Despite appearances, I'm really as good as you are, and my 'necktie,' though perhaps unconventional, is really better than your traditional tie, because it suggests the primitive and therefore the unpretentious, pure, and virtuous." Says the bola, "The person wearing me is a child of nature, even though actually eighty years old." Like many things bought by proles, these bola ties can be very expensive, especially when the slide is made of precious metal or displays "artwork." The point again is that money, although important, is not always the most important criterion of class. Below the bola wearers, at the very bottom, stand the low proles, the destitute, and the bottom-out-of-sight, who never wear a tie, or wear one—and one is all they own—so rarely that the day is memorable for that reason. Down here, the tie is an emblem of affectation and even effeminacy, and you can earn a reputation for being la-di-da by appearing in one, as if you thought yourself better than other people. One prole wife says of her spouse: "I'm going to bury my husband in his T-shirt if the undertaker will allow it."

Today, hats, because of their rarity, present an easier class problem than neckties. Since the felt fedora went out, upper-middle-class people can wear only the equivalent of parody hats—"Russian" fur, the L. L. Bean "Irish" tweed hat favored by Senator Pat Moynihan, or the floppy white fishing or tennis hat popular among the top classes despite its being favored by Franklin D. Roosevelt. Class accrues to hats now only as they declare themselves to be frivolous accessories. To take any hat seriously is to descend. Especially such novelty hats as the brown-or-black-dyed rabbit-fur fedoras affected in the early 1980s by the middle class in the Northeast and upper Midwest, who sought, at once, respectability and a touch of dash. Another hat that had considerable success with the same class was the dark-blue visored "Greek fisherman's cap" as merchandised through *The New Yorker*. When worn, this item was designed to state, "I've been to Greece and am thus well-to-do, rich enough to fly long distances on Olympic Airlines, as well as adventurous enough to relish exotic things like retsina, taramasalata, etc." But the problem with this headwear was its proletarian associations, which became even more egregious when it began appearing in versions made of black leather. Actually, only six things can be made of black leather without causing class damage to the owner: belts, shoes, handbags, gloves, camera cases, and dog leashes.

There once was a time, when Czar Nicholas and King George V wore yachting caps, when visors did not convey instant prole signals, as they do now, associated as they are not just with Greek fishermen but with workmen, soldiers, chauffeurs, policemen, railway personnel, and baseball players. Proles take to visor caps instinctively, which accounts for the vast popularity among them of what we must call simply the prole cap. This is the "baseball" cap made largely of plastic meshwork in primary colors (red, blue, yellow) with, in the rear, an open space crossed by a strap for self-adjustment: "One Size Fits All [Proles]." Regardless of the precise style of the prole cap, it seems crucial that it be ugly. It's the male equivalent of the purple acrylic slacks worn by the prole's wife, and like all items of clothing, it says something. It says to those whose expensive educations have persuaded them that the ideal of dignity is the Piazza San Marco or the Parthenon or that the ideal of the male head derives from Michelangelo's *David* or the Adam of the Sistine Chapel: "I'm as good as you are." The little strap at the rear is the significant prole feature because it demeans the buyer and user, making him do the work formerly thought the obligation of the seller, who used to have to stock numerous sizes. It's like such other prole features of the contemporary scene as the jet plane and the supermarket, where convenience for the seller is disguised by publicity and fraud to pass for convenience for the buyer. To achieve even greater ugliness, the prole will sometimes wear his cap back to front. This places the strap in full view transecting the wearer's forehead, as if pride in the one-size-fits-all gadget were motivating him to display the cap's "technology" and his own command of it. President Reagan wore a prole cap while in performance once atop a tractor in Peoria. It looked natural. And any lingering uncertainty about the class meaning of the prole cap can be resolved by a glance at the upper-middle-class L. L. Bean catalog, which, while offering all sorts of headgear, draws the line at the plastic prole cap, although it does go so far as to offer one in suede. Next to the T-shirt, the prole cap is probably the favorite place for the display of language, running all the way from rudenesses like UP YOURS to gentilities like CAROLINA TOOL AND ENGINEERING CO., BALDWIN FIL-

TERS, or PARK'S SAUSAGES. Tom Carvel's prole ice-cream-franchise holders wear prole caps with CARVEL on the front.

One might think that with the prole cap one has reached the nadir in men's headgear. But no: there are one or two steps down even from it. One is the version of the prole cap into whose visor attached plastic sun-glass lenses fold up. And below even this stooge item is the Sunbrella Hat. This erects itself on little stilts from a headband and opens and closes like an umbrella. It is some twenty inches wide, and the gores between the ribs are usually red and white. It is thoroughly "modern," the sort of idea that would occur to someone only in the latter days of the twentieth century.

Which brings up the whole matter of archaism and top-class taste. We've already seen that organic ma-terials like wool and wood outrank man-made, like nylon and Formica, and in that superiority lurks the principle of archaism as well, nylon and Formica being nothing if not up-to-date. There seems a general agree-ment, even if often unconscious, that archaism confers class. Thus the middle class's choice of "colonial" or

THE POPULAR PROLE CAP, HERE WORN BACKWARD TO
EXHIBIT THE ADJUSTO-STRAP TO ADVANTAGE

"Cape Cod" houses. Thus one reason Britain and Europe still, to Americans, have class. Thus one reason why inheritance and "old money" are such important class principles. Thus the practice among top-out-of-sight and upper classes of costuming their servants in some archaic livery, even such survivals as the white apron on the maid or, on the butler, a striped vest. It's a way of implying that the money goes back a considerable time, and that one retains the preferences and habits one learned very long ago.

What Veblen specified as the leisure class's "veneration of the archaic" shows itself everywhere: in the popularity among the upper-middle class of attending opera and classical ballet; of sending its issue to single-sex prep schools, because more unregenerate and old-style than coed ones; of traveling to view antiquities in Europe and the Middle East; of studying the "humanities" instead of, say, electrical engineering, since the humanities involve the past and studying them usually results in elegiac emotions. Even the study of law has about it this attractive aura of archaism: there's all that dog Latin, and the "cases" must all be rooted in the past. Classy people never deal with the future. That's for vulgarians like traffic engineers, planners, and inventors. Speaking of the sophisticated TV viewer's love of old black-and-white films, British critic Peter Conrad comments, "Style for us is whatever's perished, outmoded, lost." Since the upper orders possess archaism as their very own class principle—even their devotion to old clothes signals their retrograde sentiment—what can the lower orders do but fly to the new, not just to sparkling new garments but to cameras and electronic apparatus and stereo sets and trick watches and electric kitchens and video games?

As Russell Lynes perceived in *The Tastemakers*, despite the façade of modernity a corporation erects

to impress the proles, behind the scenes the upper
business classes cleave to flagrantly archaic effects.
"If you will visit Lever House in New York," he writes,

> the sheer glass box that sits handsomely on Park
> Avenue to house the offices of Lever Brothers, you
> will find that the higher the echelon the more old-
> fashioned the surroundings. The public front is one
> of daring modernity. The offices of the clerks and
> department managers are in the functional tradition.
> But when you reach the offices of top management
> you will find that there are open fireplaces and chan-
> deliers with an Early American flavor. . . . If you will
> visit the executive dining room of the J. Walter
> Thompson Company . . . you will find yourself in what
> appears to be a Cape Cod house furnished with
> Windsor chairs and rag rugs. It has wooden case-
> ment windows.

As all salesmen recognize, if you're selling something
it's better for your social class to be selling something
archaic—like real wine or unpasteurized cheese or
bread without preservatives or Renaissance art objects
or rare books. Selling something old, indeed, almost
redeems the class shame of selling anything at all. Even
trading in real sponges is class-preferable to trading in
artificial ones, a fact permitting us to appreciate the
way the organic and archaic finally fuse into one classy
thing.

It is in part because Britain has seen better days
that Anglophilia is so indispensable an element in upper-class taste, in clothes, literature, allusion, manners, and ceremony. The current irony of the
Anglophilic class motif will not escape us. In the nineteenth century, with Britain commanding much of the
world, it would seem natural for snobs to ape British
usages. Snobs still do, but not because Britain is pow-

erful but because Britain is feeble. To acquire and display British goods shows how archaic you are, and so validates upper- and upper-middle-class standing. Thus tartan skirts for women, Shetland sweaters, Harris tweeds, Burberrys, "regimental" neckties. A general American male assumption among classes above high prole is that to be "well dressed" you should look as much as possible like a British gentleman as depicted in movies about fifty years ago. One reason riding lessons are vouchsafed the young of the top classes is that the socially best outfits and accessories are imported from England. Top-class food resembles British, being bland and mushy, with little taste and no chances taken. The upper-middle-class Sunday dinner is often indistinguishable from its British counterpart: roast, with potatoes and two veg. Being the American ambassador to the Court of St. James's is still felt to confer upper-class status, even if you're really Walter Annenberg. It's not like being ambassador to Sri Lanka or Venezuela.

Deeply engraved on the American consciousness is the superstition, abundantly visible in the Gothic flourishes of our university architecture, that institutions of the higher learning are the more authentic the more they allude to their two great British originals. Thus a low mail-order degree mill in Glendale, California, searching for a name for itself that will attract maximum prole bucks, comes up with—Kensington University. But it's when you move north from the prole and middle classes and approach the upper-middle that you begin to get overpowering whiffs of Mother England, which smells like expensive old leather bindings, Jeyes's fluid, and tar soap. You realize that in the upper-middle class are people who actually believe that Oxford and Cambridge are better, rather than just older, than Harvard and Yale—and the University of

Michigan, for that matter. Examining the upper-middle class, you find people who, despite their normal proud resistance to advertising, believe that Schweppes club soda is better than White Rock. You meet people whose dinner tables ring not just with passing references to the royal family but with prolonged earnest dissertations about Charles and Lady Di and Margaret and Anne and Andrew and little Prince William.

And the appeal of Anglophilia to even the middle class should never be underestimated. I say this on the evidence of a correspondence I once had with a friend of mine, a "developer" or mass house contractor who built whole new towns at once. Having run out of names for his streets, he solicited my help. (I was living in Knightsbridge at the time.) He asked me to supply him with an alphabetical list of classy—that is, British—street names that would attract the eminently middle-class buyers of his houses. Knowing how important this was for the self-respect and even mental health of his clients, I sent him a list immediately, which started like this:

> Albemarle
> Berkeley
> Cavendish
> Devonshire
> Exeter
> Fanshawe, etc.

All he had to do was add such terminations as

> Street
> Court
> Circle
> Way

Lane (as in Park "Lane")
Grove

and his house-buyers would be spared the shame of living on McGillicutty Street or Bernstein Boulevard or Guappo Terrace. When I reached the end of the alphabet—passing through Landsdowne and Montpelier and Osborne and Priory—I couldn't resist "Windsor" for W, and today there's some poor puzzled fellow wondering why success is so slow in arriving, since for years he's been residing at 221 Windsor Close instead of living on West Broad Street. New terrible jumped-up places like Houston are quick to surround themselves with tract suburbs bearing the most egregious British names, like these (which actually are parts of Houston):

Nottingham Oaks
Afton Oaks
Inverness Forest
Sherwood Forest (!)
Braes Manor
Meredith Manor

There's even a Shamrock Manor, hardly Anglo and only very doubtfully classy, but Houston's so far from Boston that perhaps no one will catch on. It all reminds one a bit of poor Dr. Herman ("Hy") Tarnower, done to death by his upper-middle girlfriend, who hoped to disguise his vulgarity by strewing his waiting room with British periodicals.

The same sense that if it's British it must have class prompts those who change their names to opt for Anglophilic sounds. No one would change from Poshenitz to Gamberini, but all would change from Horowitz to

Howe. And if you merchandise tasteless little blobs of dough, you can sell billions of them by calling them "English" muffins.

❈[IV]❈

ABOUT THE HOUSE

WHEN IN ONE OF HIS POEMS W. H. AUDEN INDICATED that *healers* were to be found not only in city clinics but in

> country houses at the end of drives,

he was hardly suggesting that they were proles, or even middle-class. An acute reader of class signals, he knew that the sort of driveway you have, if any, suggests virtually as much about you as the house it leads to.

If you're not able to find some people's driveways at all, you are safe to infer that they're top-out-of-sight. It's only with the upper class that driveways become visible and available for study. In general, we can say that there, the longer the drive the higher the class, with the proviso that long and curved is grander than long and straight. The reason, as Veblen perceived, is that the curved driveway is more "futile," taking up more land. "The canon of futility," he notes, dictates that the best driveway is "a circuitous drive laid across level ground." (If the ground weren't level, there might be a utilitarian reason for the curve: as it is, it's pure play and show.) Even with the more modest upper-middle-class driveway, if it goes straight into the garage, it has less class than if it curves. The surface of the drive is important too. The most impressive surface you can have on an upper-middle-class driveway is gravel in some neutral or dark shade. Beige is best. White gravel is lower, violating as it does the axiom that bold effects and vivid contrasts are always to be avoided. Asphalt is lower still—too utilitarian and economical. Gravel beats asphalt not just because it's more archaic but because it must be renewed often at considerable expense and inconvenience. Because the desire for privacy is a top-class sign, high walls—anything higher than six or seven feet—confer class, while low ones, or see-through fences, or none at all, proclaim the middle class. Unless the house is known to be very splendid and is out of sight from the road, entryway gates are pretentious.

But you can be pretentious merely with the way you display your house number. One form of vainglory is to spell the number out (you can do this on stationery too), like "Two Hundred Five" ("Two Hundred and Five" is even more offensive). Or you can plaster your family name on the façade or mailbox: "The Johnsons," as if you were an institution. Or you can name your house as if it were something like Windsor Castle and blazon the name somewhere on the front: "The Willows." There's almost no limit to how cute you can be here, especially if you are upper-middle-class and fancy British usages. But in England, house-naming is also popular among proles who want to signal the message that their premises are not public housing but are owned and (largely) paid for by the occupants.

Garages: the upper-middle-class and middle-class house used to act ashamed of its garage, concealing it well in back with other unseemly outbuildings. But now the garage is very much a part of the owner's class presentation, and it's been moved forward on the lot so that passersby can appreciate its two-car size and admire its basketball backboard and hoop (evidence that the house contains at least one member of the leisure class junior grade). The more visible from the street the garage is, the more its costly trick doors can be noted and envied. Three-car and larger garages are seldom seen, not because there aren't any but because they're part of the invisible residences of the top-out-of-sights.

Approaching any house, one is bombarded with class signals. The serious student will not panic but will take them one at a time. The lawn first. Its very existence is an announcement of Anglophilia, England being the place where the lawn came into its own. Finicky neatness here is usually a sign of social anxiety, a tip-off that we are approaching middle-class premises. If there's no crabgrass at all, we can infer an owner who spends much of his time worrying about slipping down a class or two, the lawn being, as Brooks notes, "a crucial arena for classical predatory indiviousness and its concomitant, anxiety." Neglect of one's lawn in middle-class neighborhoods can invite terrible retribution. "The sanctions are not obvious," says William H. Whyte, Jr., "but the look in the eye, the absence of a smile, the inflection of a hello, can be exquisite punishment, and they have brought more than one to a nervous breakdown." If you keep an animal to crop your lawn (only the upper class does this), it's essential that it not be something useful in other ways like a sheep or cow or even a goat, creatures which, as Veblen says, have about them "the vulgar suggestion of thrift," but an animal of a more wasteful and exotic kind, like a deer, something "not vulgarly lucrative either in fact or in suggestion," and thus a happy emblem of "futility."

In cold-weather areas a problem arises for the middle class when the lawn is snow-covered and thus unavailable for invidious display. Hence the middle-class Christmas light show as a form of compensation, with reindeer prancing on the asbestos shingles, jocose Santas entering chimneys, and, on pious lawns, plywood Nativities. No one has ever sufficiently studied the middle-class determination to avoid criticism by putting on, as John Brooks says, "the biggest Christmas time light show on the block," nor sufficiently investigated the relation of the light show to "lawn care." One suburb studied by Whyte for his book *The Organization Man* (1956) goes so wild lighting up at holiday time that every year 100,000 people (proles, surely) drive through to marvel at the effects.

When the front lawn becomes a showcase for permanent objects meant to be admired, we know that we are proceeding down toward the proles. High-prole items for lawn exhibition are urns painted blinding white, as well as front-yard "trees" consisting of some fifteen green-painted wrought-iron branches, each holding, in a ring at the tip, a flower pot. Some prole lawn objects are meant to be not just admired but actually worshiped, like a statue of the Blessed Virgin, which one sees sometimes presented inside an old-fashioned claw-footed bathtub propped upright. A slightly lower kind of class statement is that made by plastic gnomes and flamingos and Disney animals, and by blue or lavender basketball-size shiny spheres resting on fluted cast-concrete pedestals. Proceeding further downward (we're now at about low prole), we see things like defunct truck tires painted white with flowers planted inside. (Auto tires are a grade higher.) At the very class bottom are flower-bed enclosures made

of rows of dead light bulbs or the butts of disused beer
bottles. Down here, another bit of front-yard décor will
be a rusty supermarket cart, waiting quietly for further
employment.

A MIDDLE-CLASS HOUSEHOLDER CONFRONTS A DAMNING
IMPURITY ON HIS LAWN

Anyone imagining that just any sort of flowers can
be presented in the front of a house without status
jeopardy would be wrong. Upper-middle-class flowers
are rhododendrons, tiger lilies, amaryllis, columbine,
clematis, and roses, except for bright-red ones. One
way to learn which flowers are vulgar is to notice the
varieties favored on Sunday-morning TV religious programs like Rex Humbard's or Robert Schuller's. There
you will see primarily geraniums (red are lower than
pink), poinsettias, and chrysanthemums, and you will

know instantly, without even attending to the quality of the discourse, that you are looking at a high-prole setup. Other prole flowers include anything too vividly red, like red tulips. Declassed also are phlox, zinnias, salvia, gladioli, begonias, dahlias, fuchsias, and petunias. Members of the middle class will sometimes hope to mitigate the vulgarity of bright-red flowers by planting them in a rotting wheelbarrow or rowboat displayed on the front lawn, but seldom with success.

Advertising is a good way to ascertain what we might call the social language of flowers. In her study of the American funeral business, *The American Way of Death* (1963), Jessica Mitford calls attention to an ad in an undertakers' trade journal celebrating the profits to be realized in the traditional collusion between the cadaver embalmer and the florist. In the ad a new young widow is being presented with some flowers, and, as the picture caption says, "Softness comes back to her face as sorrow begins to slip away." The acute reader will not need to be told that the flowers in question are—chrysanthemums.

But what of the house we are approaching? If it is relatively new it will be so commonplace and uniform and ugly that ascertaining the exact class of its owner will be difficult. A sarcastic but perhaps not unfair view of it is Russell Lynes's:

> Today's house, however expensive, has become a box..., or a series of boxes. Sometimes the box has a sharply peaked roof and is covered with white clapboards, in which case it is called a Cape Cod. If it is a box longer than it is wide and has a gently pitched roof, then it is a ranch house. If it is a square box, it is...a bungalow. If it is a two-story box, it is "colonial." If it is two boxes set next to each other but one a little above the other, then it is a split-level. (It can be either a split-level Cape Cod or a split-level ranch.)

That is the upper-middle-class and middle-class house. The upper-class version will be set back farther from the street, but if built in the last twenty-five years it will be essentially little different. The prole model, on the other hand, will be identifiable less because it's smaller than because of the power boat, trailer, or "recreational vehicle" exhibited in the driveway, which will be, of course, straight and asphalted. This in addition to the one or more moribund automobiles disposed about the premises. These are more authentic if elevated on concrete blocks. If you remove these driveway or backyard vehicles and instead plant a fake white wooden well-house in the front yard, you instantly, all other things being equal, transform the prole house into middle-class. This well-house is a component of the New England look, which is one form taken by the snob archaizing impulse of the middles. Other elements of the New England look are brass or black-painted "coach" lanterns on either side of the front door, with a similar lamp on a tall white post to illuminate the front walk; a weather vane on a detachable white cupola imposed on the roof of the garage; and a gilded or black "colonial" eagle above the front door: it will be made of cast aluminum but painted to ape hand-carved wood. There seems no house too mean to display the eagle, although it gradually seems to be losing its power to convey the snob message "Early America": one upper-middle-class friend of mine who had noticed a lot of these eagles on rather mean little houses thought they designated the residences of naval aviators. Other archaic house styles favored by the middle class are the model imitating the nineteenth-century American farmhouse (virtuous and cozy) and the "Tudor," with a brave show of half-timber work on the front (solid, impeccably trustworthy).

Given the structural uniformity of the boxes constituting the current house, the owner must depend largely on front-porch and façade appliqués and decorations (like the eagle) to deliver the news about the social status he's claiming. In the 1950s this used to be the social function of both rooftop television aerials and protruding window air conditioners, but now of course both transmit entirely unhonorific status messages. The front porch and doorway area are to the house what the mouth is to the human face, like the mouth conveying ungainsayable class signals. Whether high or low, the domestic façade labors to extort respect, and it is thus one of the most pathetic of artifacts, bespeaking the universal human need to claim dignity and high consequence.

One middle-class way of doing this is through "neoclassic" effects of absolute symmetry, of the sort achieved by a potted small tree on either side of the front door or by the well-known emblem of the precisely equal side curtains pulled back from the ranch-house picture window to reveal a table lamp, the cellophane on its shade visibly inviolate, positioned exactly in the middle of a centered table. A similar symmetrical effect (saying, "We are instinctively neat") is aimed at by installing two outdoor chairs (metal, with pipe arms) as a "conversation group" on the front porch, in stubborn defiance of the traffic thundering past. The middle-class longing for dignity frequently expresses itself in columns or pilasters arguing the impressive weight of the edifice. In one model of a middle-class house, these often attenuate to mere white-painted sticks (four of them, usually) two stories tall, supporting a flyweight rooflet extending over the façade of a Tara-like "Southern mansion." This sort of fraudulent support is endemic in the middle-class dwelling, and it's visible in a socially slightly lower form in two massive square brick pillars holding up a

light porch roof, or in obese porch columns made of
large boulders stuck together with mortar, or in heavy
wrought-iron supports pretending to be needed to prevent a thirty-pound jalousie from crashing to the ground.

Near where I live there's a middle-class house which
beautifully illustrates the dangerous proximity of dignity to pomposity. The house is actually a modest bun-
galow, a one-story gray box covered with asbestos
"shakes" and topped by a simple peaked roof. It looks
very like a one-story army barracks—nothing at all
fancy in the basic fabric. But the owner, gnawed by
folie de grandeur, has equipped it with a fake brick
front, with, on each side of the front door, white fluted
Ionic columns holding up nothing at all. (The principle
that curves are classier than straight lines operates with
columns as with driveways, and has been understood
by this aspirant. Square columns are the lowest; round
ones the next highest; round and fluted highest of all.)
Against this man's fake, bright-red brick facing we find
a maximum of "colonial" white trim as a vivid contrast—sills, shutters, canopies, etc. The house begs
the observer on no account to look at its honest sides
and rear but only at its front. It nicely illustrates
Veblen's acute point about the apartment houses built
in his time: "The needless variety of fronts presented
by the better class of tenements and apartment houses
in our cities is an endless variety of architectural distress.
... Considered as objects of beauty, the dead walls of
the sides and back of these structures, left untouched
by the hands of the artist, are commonly the best feature of the building."

Bright red juxtaposed with blinding white somehow
connote elegance in that social place where middle
class meets high prole. I'm thinking of a high-prole
little house I know in a small city. It's sited very close
to the sidewalk and approached by a short concrete

stairway. On either side of the stairway is a small lion *couchant* made of cast concrete. The two lions are painted dead white with their mouths picked out in brightest red. You feel that some sort of quasi-"heraldic" message is being aimed at, although ascertaining exactly what it is would engage a staff of semioticians for some weeks. Another way of achieving the red-and-white effect is to paint the bricks bright red and the mortar pure white. You're likely to come upon this where you also see such prole signals as what can be called the Sheraton Effect—the front steps (three at least) covered with brilliant green outdoor carpeting, very neatly applied, with razor-sharp edges and hospital corners. On high-prole porches there will usually be a "glider," although on low-prole porches the back-seat removed from an old auto will serve. The point is to have something to court on. And in Southern states there will be a refrigerator on the front porch, its curious position perhaps owing something to the nineteenth-century tradition that the proper place for the ice box is the back porch, so that the iceman (a member of a yet lower class) can be excluded from the house proper. The refrigerator on the prole front porch serves two purposes: it announces to passersby that you own a costly appliance, and it contains items you need to consume while courting on the glider—"soda" (or "dopes"), fruit, and similar refreshments.

Walking now around behind the house, we should consider the way windows manifest social standing. The principle applying is, as usual, archaism. Socially, the highest kind of windows are pseudo-eighteenth-century wooden sash windows, and the more panes per sash, the better: six is standard, twelve, distinguished. One would think that the archaistic principle would confer great class on the mock-Tudor leaded window with diamond-shaped panes, but it doesn't:

these windows are too palpably fraudulent, theatrical, and Camp, simply absurd, like collegiate or church Gothic architecture, in a country founded only in the eighteenth century. Some proles aim for status by going in for "portholes" on their split-level ranch houses, circular openings a foot and a half in diameter with white surrounds suggesting archaic life rings. By this means they hope to suggest time spent in yachts. Few will be deceived. If you have storm windows fitted over your sash windows, for class purposes the wooden ones are better than metal, both because they honor the organic-materials principle and because, on a large house, they seem to presuppose a servant (or "outdoor man") to put them up and take them down.

If there were such he'd also be in charge of the outdoor furniture around in back. Organic materials are important here, dictating that the lowest you can sink is to folding chairs made of aluminum tubing with bright-green plastic-mesh webbing which, with wear, grows gradually looser. Wooden furniture is probably the classiest, with plenty of overstuffed cushions, for it's a top-class principle never (except on a yacht) to be in the slightest degree uncomfortable. If you wouldn't sit on stretched vinyl strips indoors, why do it outside? If there's a patio, for class purposes it should be much larger than needed, and on it should stand a table with a glass top. The glass should be clear, not wrinkled, for clear glass, being harder to keep clean, suggests a servant to clean it—hence, by the way, the desirability of lots of mirrors indoors. Breakfast at this clear-glass-topped table on the extra-large patio is an upper-class or upper-middle-class practice established by the films of the 1940s and 1950s. At a table like this, you sit on white wrought-iron chairs equipped with deep cushions, and you drink orange juice, freshly squeezed, of course, but certainly not by yourself. (White-painted wrought iron is one of the few permissible deviations from the organic-materials principle.)

The automobile, like the all-important domestic façade, is another mechanism for outdoor class display. Or class lack of display we'd have to say, if we focus on the usages of the upper class, who, on the principle of archaism, affect to regard the automobile as very *nouveau* and underplay it consistently. Class understatement describes the technique: if your money and freedom and carelessness of censure allow you to buy any kind of car, you provide yourself with the meanest and most common to indicate that you're not taking seriously so easily purchasable and thus vulgar a class totem. You have a Chevy, Ford, Plymouth, or Dodge, and in the least interesting style and color. It may be clean, although slightly dirty is best. But it should be boring. The next best thing is to have a "good" car, like a Jaguar or BMW, but to be sure it's old and beat-up. You may not have a Rolls, a Cadillac, or a Mercedes. Especially a Mercedes, a car, Joseph Epstein reports in *The American Scholar* (Winter 1981–82), which the intelligent young in West Germany regard, quite correctly, as "a sign of high vulgarity, a car of the kind owned by Beverly Hills dentists or African cabinet ministers." The worst kind of upper-middle-class types own Mercedes, just as the best own elderly Oldsmobiles, Buicks, and Chryslers, and perhaps Jeeps and Land Rovers, the latter conveying the Preppy suggestion that one of your residences is in a place so unpublic that the roads to it are not even paved, indeed are hardly passable by your ordinary vulgar automobile. And the understatement canon determines that the higher your class, the slower you drive. Speeders are either young non-Anglo-Saxon high-school proles hoping to impress girls of a similar sort, or insecure, status-anxious middle-class men who have seen too many movies involving auto chases and as a result think cars romantic, sexy, exciting, etc. The requirements of class dictate that you drive slowly, steadily, and silently, and as near the middle of the road as possible.

The class expressiveness of a car doesn't stop with the kind and condition of car it is, or with the way you drive it. It involves also the things you display on or in it, all the way from the rack holding three rifles, shotguns, or carbines in the rear window of the pickup with the Southern Methodist University sticker to the upper-middle-class rear-window announcement "I'd Rather Be Sailing." Proles love to decorate their cars, not just with mock-leopard upholstery and things like dice and baby shoes dangling from front and rear windows but with bumper stickers (AUSABLE CHASM; SOUTH OF THE BORDER; AYATOLLAH—PIG'S ASSHOLAH; HONK IF YOU LOVE JESUS), and of course little plastic Saint Christophers and the like on the dashboard. The middle class likes bumper stickers too, but is more likely to go in for self-congratulatory messages like CAUTION: I BRAKE FOR SMALL ANIMALS.

Americans are the only people in the world known to me whose status anxiety prompts them to advertise their college and university affiliations in the rear windows of their automobiles. You can drive all over Europe without once seeing a rear-window sticker reading CHRIST CHURCH or UNIVERSITÉ DE PARIS. A convention in the United States is that the higher learning is so serious a matter that joking or parody are wholly inappropriate. Actually, there's hardly an artifact more universally revered by Americans of all classes than the rear-window college sticker. One would sooner defile the flag than mock the sticker or what it represents by, say, putting it on upside down or slantwise, or scratching ironic quotation marks around "College" or "University." I have heard of one young person who cut apart and rearranged the letters of his STANFORD sticker so that his rear window said SNODFART. But the very rarity of so scandalous a performance is significant. And no family fortunate enough to be associated with Harvard or Princeton, no matter how remotely, would fly a KUTZTOWN STATE COLLEGE sticker as an ironic jest. These stickers pose an ethical problem uniquely American: how long after a family member has ceased to attend a classy college may one display the sticker? One year? Ten years? Forever? The American family would appreciate some authoritative guidance here, perhaps from the colleges themselves.

THE PROLE AUTOMOBILE, REAR VIEW

Just as you generally don't joke with the college sticker, you don't joke with the furnishing and decorating of the rooms of the house likely to be seen by strangers. Especially the living room, "the family's best foot a few inches forward, or sometimes a few miles," as Russell Lynes says. An upper-middle-class and often a middle-class house can be identified immediately you're inside by the way it stints the space allotted to the bedrooms and backstage areas so that the living room can constitute a more ample theater of display. The kinds of cultural emblems exhibited there were the focus of an elaborate study by sociologist F. Stuart Chapin almost fifty years ago in his book *Contemporary American Institutions* (1935). "The attitude of friends and other visitors, and hence social status," as he said, "may be advantageously influenced by the selection and proper display of cultural objects in the living room." To assist in measuring the class message projected by a living room, Chapin devised what he called "The Living-Room Scale," awarding or subtracting points for various items exhibited. Thus, if you had an alarm clock in your living room, you forfeited 2 points, but if you had a "fireplace with three or more utensils," you gained 8. A hardwood floor brought you 10, each curtained window 2, each bookcase with books 8. Each displayed newspaper and magazine earned 8, but a sewing machine, if you were so thoughtless as to position it in your living room, cost you 2. Admirable as this idea is, there are a couple of weaknesses in it. Chapin's distinctions, for one thing, aren't fine enough. The displayed magazines, for example: it matters terribly what magazines they are. A *Reader's Digest* and a *Family Circle* should lower you considerably on the scale, but they can be counterbalanced by display of a *Smithsonian* or *Art News*. And secondly, Chapin failed to take into account the practice among some upper-middles of parody display, a practice which has advanced dramatically since his day. All the regrettable items he notices, including even the sewing machine, could be advantageously exhibited today in a Camp or hi-tech-parody setting. I have tried to bring Chapin's Living-Room Scale up to date and make it a more trustworthy gauge for measuring the social class of your neighbors and friends. You'll find my version in the Appendix of this book.

The upper-class living room is very likely to have

an eleven-to-thirteen-foot ceiling, to contain wasteful curves—moldings on baseboards, door panels, and the like—and, if wood is visible, to feature dark rather than light wood (more archaic-looking). There must be a hardwood floor—parquet is best—covered, but not entirely, with Orientals so old as to be almost threadbare, suggesting inheritance from a primeval past. (On the other hand, a new Oriental, no matter how visibly expensive, is an all but infallible middle-class sign.) In the upper-class living room there may be exquisite homemade petit-point chair seats or a brick doorstop covered in needlepoint—these suggest yards and yards of leisure on the part of the lady of the house. In general, the more allusions to European architectural décor, the higher the class: black-and-white marble entryways, balustrades and railings, brocaded wall coverings, brass door fittings (which imply daily polishing by someone, certainly not the owner)—all confer the air both of archaism and the un-American so essential for upper-class status. There is one item which, although not indispensable in an upper-class setting, is never found outside one. It's the tabletop obelisk made of marble or crystal, a sly allusion not to Egypt —there would be no class there—but to Paris. And also to Tiffany, known by the cognoscenti to be the main local outlet for these choice items. And flowers usually appear in upper living rooms. (*Fresh flowers*, the middle-class housewife will call them, to distinguish them from the plastic ones assumed in her world.)

As we move down a bit to the upper-middle class, certain features begin to enter the picture. Like the middlebrow "oil portrait" of the head of the household or his wife or issue, executed by someone like Zita Davisson, "the noted portrait artist . . . celebrated throughout the world for her realistic, expressive style." You can book a sitting with her through Bergdorf-

Goodman. If that's too costly, you can display a photographic portrait of yourself (as if you were Churchill)
made by Yousuf Karsh, who advertises in *The New
Yorker*. If you put it in an easel frame, the frame must
be of silver, like the cedar-lined cigarette box on the
coffee table. If your living room has come equipped
with more bookcases than you need, you can always
respond to the ad of a company called itself Books by
the Yard (601 Madison Avenue, New York City):
"Leather Bound Books, 18th and 19th Century Fiction,
Biography, Ecclesiastic, Essays, Shakespeare, Field-
ing, Carlyle, Swift, Pope, Johnson, Milton, etc....
Excellent source for interior decorators." In the genuine upper-middle-class living room nautical allusions
will be visible somewhere, like a framed map of Nantucket, implying intimate familiarity with its waters. In
this class, the Orientals will be worn but not threadbare.

If the living rooms of the top classes tend to ape art
galleries and museums, those of the middle class and
below resemble motel rooms. Socially crucial is the
dividing line where original works of art or *virtu* are
replaced by reproductions. The Tiffany lamp is a case
in point. It lost caste fatally the moment reproductions
with plastic "glass" began showing up in middle-class
houses and restaurants, and now one sees the things
even in prole settings. The middle-class living room
may display "louvers" somewhere, and the furniture
(most likely in the "colonial" style) will be of maple or
pine. There may be cute wall plates at the light
switches—porcelain, with flowers, cartoon characters,
imitation samplers, etc.—and hanging against a wall
you may find a rack soliciting admiration for a vast
"collection" of outré items like match folders or swiz-
zle sticks. The floor will be carpeted wall to wall, and
there will be venetian blinds made not of wood but of

metal, with the slats curved. If potted plants are displayed, there may be cactuses among them.

But the most notable characteristic of middle-class décor is the flight from any sort of statement that might be interpreted as "controversial" or ideologically pointed. One can't be too careful. Pictures, for example: safe are sailing vessels, small children and animals, and pastoral scenes, unlike images that hint any ideological import, like "France," "Civil War," "New York City," or "East European Immigration." Argument or even disagreement must be avoided at all costs. In aid of this high-minded end, benign mottos and signs are useful, like the favorite which reads,

> Great Spirit, grant that I may not criticize my neighbor until I have walked a mile in his moccasins.

Audubon prints on the wall are nicely nonideological, and "wall systems" are popular because they are more likely to contain stereos and TVs than bookshelves, always a danger because they may display books with controversial spines. In the same way your real middle class refuses to show any but the most bland books and magazines on its coffee tables: otherwise, expressions of opinion, awkward questions, or even ideas might result. Thus in lieu of conversation, the photographic slide show—a pleasantly nonideological middle-class fixture, almost as welcome as an antidote to ideas as the *National Geographic* itself. The middle-class anxiety about ideology is strongly implied by a phrase popular among the middles, "good taste," which means, as Russell Lynes notes, the "entirely inoffensive and essentially characterless." (To do your living room in "good taste" you go to W. & J. Sloan in New York or Marshall Field in Chicago.) One reason for the absence of character in middle-class decorating is that the women get their ideas from national magazines and assume, as one woman told Lynes, that "if you've seen something in a magazine—well, people will nearly always like it." Hence the brass skillet hung against the brick wall, the "colonial" wallpaper, etc. And it's true too that much of this characterlessness can be imputed to the frequency with which the middle class is moved from suburb to suburb by the corporations which employ it. What works in one house must work in the next. As one middle-class wife told Vance Packard, "I settle for something that will move well."

To change a middle-class living room to a prole one, you'd add a Naugahyde Barcalounger and reinvite ideology back into the pictures, but the ideology would be the sort conveyed in the popular chromo "Christ at the United Nations." Thick transparent plastic would cover the upholstery, fringe would appear around the bottom of the sofa, and little woolly balls would dangle from the lampshades, which might be tied with large bows. These things would satisfy the prole hunger for, as decorators put it, "lots of goop." The dining table would be of metal and Formica, and somewhere a bowling-ball carrier might be visible.

An observer with little time to spend in a house can make a fair estimate of the class of the occupants by noting the position of the TV set. The principle is that the higher in class you are, the less likely it is that your TV will be exhibited in your living room. Openly and proudly, that is: if you want it there for convenience or because there's no other place to put it, you'll drain away some of its nastiness by an act of parody display—indicating that you're not taking the TV at all seriously by using the top as a shelf for ridiculous objects like hideous statuettes, absurd souvenirs, hilariously awful wedding presents, and the like.

(This is assuming you have a TV at all. The upper

class tends not to. In a recent book of one hundred photographs of upper-class people in their houses in Lake Forest, Illinois, only one TV set is to be seen. TV is distinctly, as one industry spokesman said recently, "not a patrician medium," and it's a startling

TV SET DISARMED OF SOME OF ITS NASTINESS BY PARODY DISPLAY

fact that there are upper-class people who've never heard of Lucy or the Muppets.)

An upper-middle-class way to devulgarize the set is to have it gussied up to look like something else, like "fine furniture" or a Gothic drinks cabinet in "valuable woods." Or you can have it hidden behind a two-way mirror, or behind a painting, which can slide up on tracks when it's necessary to disclose the small screen. Or, as the British critic Peter Conrad observes, "Often in highbrow households the set will be found snugly lodged in a wall of bookshelves, as if proximity could make an erzatz literary object of it."

Down among the middles and high proles the set ceases to be an occasion of shame and becomes instead a specific glory of the family. Here you find sets flaunting their complicated technology, with control panels looking like fixtures from jet aircraft or space capsules. Here also you're likely to find two or more sets (color, of course), and the further down socially you proceed the more likely that they'll be on all the time. In fact, if you're in the presence of one or more sets that are seldom dark, you're either a prole, someone who works in the TV or news industry, someone who does public relations for the President of the United States, or a person who runs an appliance store. Among mid- and low proles, the set will probably be found in the dining room or kitchen, wherever the family gathers for meals. This allows the TV to replace conversation entirely, which is why these classes depend upon it.

And of course what you watch on the set betrays your class at once. Or don't watch, for the upper-middle class, those whose sets are disguised as something else, watches little more than an occasional emission from National Educational Television or a news special, like coverage of the current political assassination. The middle class likes *M*A*S*H* and *All* *in the Family*, with the occasional dose of *Paper Chase*, but what it prefers most is sports viewing, although *viewing*'s not precisely the right word. That's what you'd be doing if you were present at the game. TV sports watching is "Indirect Spectatorism," as Roger Price says. "Someone else," he comments rather severely, "is even doing our *watching* for us." And of course the more violent the body contact of the sports you watch, the lower your class. Tennis and golf and even bowling are classier to watch than boxing, hockey, and pro football. TV news is also watched regularly by the middle class, the audience that deified Walter Cronkite and whose loyalty to the seven-o'clock news, even if that snotty Dan Rather is reading it, is the main cause of the death of afternoon papers all over the country.

The bottom stratum of the middle class, together with the high proles, furnishes the audience for game shows, from the higher (like *Family Feud*), with their fairly sophisticated sexiness and venturesome jokes, to the lower (like *Tic Tac Dough*), with their nonhumiliating questions and nonthreatening emcees. The uglier the gamemaster, the greater appeal of the show to proles. *Blockbusters* is an illustration. There's no chance of being patronized or put down by a person so unprepossessing as the just-folks emcee Bill Cullen, whose polyester clothes in addition make him seem quite one of us proles.

The lower proles will watch any of this stuff on occasion, because as long as the set's on and playing, they're moderately satisfied, pleased with the subliminal message their TV's always conveying: "I Am Owned by a Family That Can Afford a Color TV." On their ostentatiously technological sets, mid- and low proles like to watch sitcoms based either on outright magic (*The Flying Nun*) or on some technological marvel (*The Hulk, The Bionic Woman, The Six Million*

Dollar Man). The Hulk's emanating from an overdose
of gamma radiation (whatever that may be) is as attractive to proles as Superman's association with
"Kryptonite." Science and technology have never quite
made it socially (whatever Sebastian Flyte was studying at Oxford in *Brideshead Revisited*, it wasn't chemistry), partly, I suppose, because excitement over
them—and the illusion of "progress" they propose—
is a prole characteristic. Mid- and low proles also like
sitcoms like *Love Boat* and *Gilligan's Island* with dialogue so untaxing that no one in the viewing family
will be embarrassed by not getting it. Close to the
bottom as a class indicator is *The Flintstones*, appealing as it does to the audience that takes in a paper
only for the funnies. Watching news or sports interviews on TV, you doubtless have seen people, not all
of them adolescents, who carefully position themselves
just in the background and jump up and down and wave
frantically while wearing theatrically broad smiles.
Hoping to be distinguished if only for a moment by
being caught by "a media" and recognized—glory!—
by family and friends, they reveal that they are low
proles.

Because most mid- and low proles work under supervision and hate it, they identify readily with TV
characters in similar predicaments, harassed like the
viewer by superintendents and foremen and inspec-
tors. One reason police shows are popular is that they
involve such appealing elements as brutality and coercion, but they're popular also because the prole viewer
can identify himself easily with characters who are
constantly either disobeying a boss, "getting around
him," or humoring him. Likewise with newspaper
shows like *Lou Grant* and "employee" dramas like
Alice and *Nine to Five*.

Proles like TV commercials. At times their conver-

sation consists of little more than allusions to them: "I
can't believe I ate the whole thing"; "Don't leave home
without them"; "How do *you* spell relief?" Bottom-
out-of-sights love TV, but the choice of what to watch
belongs largely to institutional personnel like prison
guards or nurses and orderlies at establishments for
the senile. In prison any show is popular which depicts
luscious girls and stimulates imagery of having to do
with them. As one former inmate told Studs Terkel,
"Your whole day was sitting in a room...watching
television. *The Dating Game* was a big hit because it
dealt with women."

So much for the living room and its main giveaway
piece of furniture, the TV. Although the living room
is the most important conveyor of class signals, two
other rooms should not be neglected, the kitchen and
the bathroom. The upper-class kitchen, designed to be
entered only by servants, is identifiable at once: it's
beat-up, inconvenient, and out-of-date, with lots of
wood, no Formica whatever, and a minimum of accessories and labor-saving appliances like dishwashers
and garbage disposals. Why tolerate these noisy things
when you can have a silent servant do precisely what
they do? The upper-class kitchen does have a refrigerator, but so antique that it has rounded corners and
a big white coil on top. Neatness and modernity enter
as we move down toward the middle class, and the
more your kitchen resembles a lab, the worse for you
socially. An electric stove has less class than a gas
one, the appearance of modernity and efficiency, here
as everywhere, severely compromising one's status
presentation. The "tech" kitchen, with lots of microwave and toaster ovens and coffeemakers, is socially
as fatal as the TV set whose control panel suggests a
youth misspent at a technical institute.

The bathroom: the upper-class one will resemble

the upper-class kitchen in its backwardness. A toilet seat in dark varnished wood is class-eloquent, and so is the absence of a shower, the latter deprivation being especially valuable because of its allusion to England. Two items infallibly found in top-class bathrooms, the Mason Pearson hairbrush and the Kent comb, are trustworthy status emblems, as expressive in their way as the scented toilet paper and pink acrylic johnny-rug of the middle class.

The high-prole bathroom reveals two contradictory impulses at war: one is the desire to exhibit a "hospital" standard of cleanliness, which means splashing a lot of Lysol or Pine Oil around; the other is to display as much fanciness and luxury as possible, which means a lurch in the opposite direction, toward fur toilet seat covers and towels which don't work not merely because they are made largely of Dacron but also because a third of the remaining threads are "gold." The prole bathroom is a place for enacting the fantasy "What I'd Do If I Were Really Rich." It's a conventional show-case for a family's aspirations toward the finer things, like chrome plate, flounces and furbelows, magazine racks, gadgets and shelves, bottles and jars, creams, unguents, and lotions, with perhaps Water-Piks and electric toothbrushes thrown in as well. For dolling up the high-prole bathroom, Woolworth's sells a complete set of color-matched vinyl ruglets, one for the toilet lid, one for the toilet seat, one for the surrounding floor, and one for the top of the toilet tank, in case you should want to sit up there. For high proles the bathroom is a serious place, and you're not likely to encounter jocular display there, like toilet paper imprinted with lewd verses or simulacra of U.S. bank-notes. The water in the toilet is likely to be bright blue or green, a testimony to the resourcefulness and quick response to advertising of the housewife.

In domestic settings whether upper or prole, domestic animals are bound to be in attendance, and like everything else they give off class signals. Dogs first. They are classier the more they allude to nonutilitarian hunting, and thus to England. Top dogs consequently are Labradors, golden retrievers, corgis, King Charles spaniels, and Afghan hounds. To be upper-class you should have a lot of them, and they should be named after the costlier liquors, like Brandy and Whiskey. The middle class goes in for Scotties and Irish setters, often giving them Scottish or Irish names, although it reserves "Sean" (sometimes spelled "Shawn" to make sure everyone gets it) for its own human issue. Proles, for their part, like breeds that can be conceived to furnish "protection": Doberman pinschers, German shepherds, or pit bulls. Or breeds useful in utilitarian outdoor pursuits, like beagles. The thinness of dogs is often a sign of their social class. "Upper-class dogs," says Jilly Cooper, "have only one meal a day and are therefore quite thin, like their owners." She perceives too that classy people often affect certain breeds of dogs just because the classes below can't pronounce them. Thus their commitment to Rottweilers and Weimaraners. Dogs are popular with the top classes not just because, if large and rowdy especially, they convey the message that their owner is a member of the landed gentry, or what passes for it here. They're also popular among the uppers for the reason Jean-Jacques Rousseau indicated over two hundred years ago when he was talking with James Boswell about dogs versus cats as pets:

ROUSSEAU: Do you like cats?
BOSWELL: No.
ROUSSEAU: I was sure of that. It is my test of character. There you have the despotic instinct of men. They do

available, and pronounceable, while remaining foreign enough to qualify as a conspicuous import and thus a high-class item. Frascati is another favorite. Asking for Perrier (upper) or club soda (middle), while others are consuming alcohol, delivers a message similar to asking for white wine. It says: "I am grand and desirable for two reasons: first, I used to drink heavily, and thus formerly was funny, careless, adventuresome, etc.; and second, I had the sense to give it up, and am thus both intelligent and disciplined. Further, I am at the moment your social superior, because, sober, I'm watching you get drunk, and I can assure you that you are a pathetic spectacle."

In addition to white wine and carbonated water, other top-class drinks are vodka, especially mixed with water only—having it with tonic is a bit middle-class; Bloody Marys (but never after 3:00 P.M.); and Scotch, especially on the rocks or with a tiny bit of water. Putting soda in Scotch is thought rather coarse. Anglophilia determines that Scotch is higher than bourbon, preeminently the tipple of the middle class. That class also provides the main body of martini enthusiasts. It thinks it clever to call this drink the *martooni*. If you drink martinis *after* dinner, you are a prole. Beer is college-boy, and an acute student of this subject should be able to infer fairly accurately the class of your college by observing whether you drink Molson's, Beck's, Heineken's (a "greenie," in the idiom), or Grolsch, on the one hand, or Bud, Michelob, Stroh's, Piel's, or Schlitz, on the other, a distinction hinted at by Dwight Macdonald when he observed, commenting on the world envisaged by John O'Hara, that "a Yale man gets drunk in a wholly different way from a Penn State man." (This distinction is also a way of recognizing that, all else being equal, bottles are classier than cans— the principle of archaism again.) The middle class can be recognized by its propensity to hide the liquor in the kitchen, whence emerge the drinks slowly and grudgingly. If bottles are visible, they'll most likely be class brands like Old Grand-Dad and Tanqueray (the latter a useful Anglophilic gesture). Uppers, not requiring the internal morale support provided by brand names, serve cheap house brands with no apology. They are likely also to serve drinks in throwaway plastic glasses, the alcohol, not the accessories, being the important thing. Among the upper-middle class, on the other hand, your drink will come in an outsized old-fashioned glass imprinted in color with ducks or setters or sloops. The middle class is likely to serve drinks in

DRINKS OF THE CLASSES: LEFT, THE UPPER-MIDDLE SCOTCH AND WATER; CENTER, THE MIDDLE-CLASS BOURBON AND GINGER, WITH DECORATIONS AND CUTESIES; RIGHT, HIGH-PROLE BEER IN LEGIBLE VESSEL WHICH REPLACES THE CAN ON SPECIAL OCCASIONS

pink goblets, cut (or rather pressed) in busy patterns. High proles will use what used to be called juice glasses. You get them at the hardware or dime store, and they're decorated with oranges, strawberries, piglets, or little girls wearing sunbonnets. Jelly and peanut-butter jars with the labels soaked off are the glassware of mid- and low proles.

But the ultimate class bifurcation based on drink is simpler than that, and it cuts straight across the center of society, unmistakably dividing the top classes from the bottom. I'm speaking about the difference between dry and sweet. If the locution "a Seven and Seven" is strange to you, if your nose wrinkles a bit at the idea of drinking a shot of Seagram's Seven Crown mixed with Seven-Up, you are safely at or near the top, or at least not deeply compromised by the sugar fixation of the bottom. Bourbon "and ginger" is another drink favored down there but virtually unknown higher up. Both these, like daiquiris and stinger mists, brandy Alexanders and sweet manhattans, are often consumed *before dinner*, suggesting that the apéritif principle is not well understood except by non-proles who have undertaken extensive, i.e., European, travels.

To a startling degree, prole America is about sweet. According to the Roper poll, 40 percent of Americans (most of them proles, of course) consume at least one cola (or similar) drink every day, and proles will hardly touch bread unless it has sugar, or honey, in it. Things seem to grow worse in the Middle West, where at bars brandy often outsells whiskey, and dry wine is very hard to come by. Actually, you could probably draw a trustworthy class line based wholly on the amount of sugar consumed by a family, making allowances for the number of children in the household. Sweet alcoholic drinks are favored by the young and callow of all classes, a taste doubtless representing a transitional stage in the passage from the soda fountain to maturity. There seems something significant in the testimony of the girlfriend of Trent Lehman, the former child TV drama star who hanged himself. "He started to drink heavily, Seagram's and Seven-Up," she reports. "One day he was sitting in the Jacuzzi with all his clothes on, drunk." How like a boy. A man would have been drunk on dry white wine.

Thus when we see the TV ad commending a cracker because it's made with "A Touch of Honey," we know that either adult proles or kiddies of all classes are the audience being solicited. Or we should know: actually, not enough work has been done on the connection between eating and class. One trustworthy investigator here is Diane Johnson, who recently reviewed twenty-four cookbooks and books about food and food presentation in *The New York Review of Books*. These books were addressed to the upper-middle class, and their common emphasis, Johnson found, was on "elegance." When you give a dinner party for friends, the minute they sit at the table they cease to be friends, or even equals. They become an audience, and it's now your obligation to impress them with the grandeur or sophistication of the arrangements and the cuisine and thus establish your class superiority. Johnson infers from all this harping on elegance that "the social divisions in American life ... seem to be widening." And not only that: class anxiety seems to be increasing as well. "Here eating is not the thing," Johnson infers from these books. "[These] glossy and expensive volumes announce anxiety," fear that the status of the host may not really be securely anchored, anxiety lest it come further unfixed by negligent management of the table and the food. Thus the presence of plenty of candles, flowers, costly linens, silver candelabra and salt and pepper shakers, or better, salt in little silver dishes, with midget spoons alongside. Thus also the deployment of a multitude of superfluous wine accessories: a basket for the bottle to repose in, even though it's from the local liquor store and contains a pasteurized liquid that will not throw a sediment in a hundred years; a silver pouring spout to insert in the neck of the bottle, lest a drop of the valuable vintage be lost; trick silver-plated corkscrews; silver bottle-bottom cozies in lacy patterns; and silver coasters to set the wine glasses on.

Things like that would be deployed on the table at around 8:00 P.M., the time at which the evening meal is eaten being a remarkably trustworthy indication of class, actual or hoped-for. More so, actually, than the presence or absence on the table of items like ketchup bottles or ashtrays shaped like little toilets enjoining the diners to "Put Your Butts Here." Destitutes and bottom-out-of-sights eat dinner at 5:30, for the prole staff which takes care of them wants to clean up and be out roller skating or bowling early in the evening. It eats, thus, at 6:00 or 6:30. The family of Jack and Sophie Portnoy ate at 6:00, an indication of the prole pull on them despite his having a middle-class job, barely, that of an insurance salesman. The prole dinner can be identified not just by the time it takes place but by the time it takes to eat it. Like eight minutes from start to finish, from canned grapefruit to instant Sanka with sugar in it. Because the prole dinner is not an occasion for conversational speculation or commentary or fantasy, it can go very rapidly. It's a mere nutritional operation, although on ceremonial occasions like Christmas, Easter, or Passover, when you will bring out "the good paper napkins," it may drag out a bit. And the lower your class, the more likely that your dinner-table life will take place all year long with relatives only. This is probably less the result of poverty than fear—fear of committing class solecisms. Unless you're class-secure, you stay within what sociologists call "the kin network."

Dining "by candlelight" and other archaistic devices for prolonging the time spent at the table are left to the middle classes and above. Candles, after all, make little sense if you're eating in full daylight. The middle class eats at 7:00 or even 7:30, the upper-middle at 8:00 or 8:30. Some upper-middles, uppers, and top-out-of-sights dine at 9:00 or even later, after nightly protracted cocktail sessions lasting at least two hours. Sometimes they forget to eat at all. But the more decent and considerate upper-class people eat around 8:00 or close to that hour, being thoughtful enough not to require the staff to stay up till all hours afterward. You can identify the *nouveaux riches* by their practice of drinking until 10:00, eating until 1:30, and dismissing the cleaners-up at 3:00.

At the very top, the food is usually not very good, tending, like the conversation, to a terrible blandness, a sad lack of originality and cutting edge. Throughout his pitiable book *Live a Year with a Millionaire*, Cornelius Vanderbilt Whitney records memorable meals, and they sound like this: "Crab bisque, then chicken with ham biscuits, Bibb lettuce salad, and finally a huge...ice cream cake." This man, who could eat anything in the world he might fancy, from elephant cutlets to sorbets doused with rose water and garnished with little flakes of gold leaf, carefully records meals like this: "Delicious dinner of fried chicken, green peas, salad, and freshly baked cake." Or for breakfast: "Orange juice, half grapefruit, oatmeal, scrambled eggs, bacon, and coffee."

Gestures toward exoticism—i.e., the foreign—enter when we move down to the upper-middle class, the

style of which is aspired to by the middle-class girl who
has come to the city and whose *vade mecum* is *The
New Yorker*. Her ambitions in the cuisine are described
by Roger Price:

> After a few months in the city, prompted by econ-
> omy and boredom she learns to make a Specialty,
> always an exotic concoction much too advanced for
> her tiny kitchen: paella, an authentic curry, quiche
> Lorraine, roast beef with Yorkshire pudding. When
> entertaining... beaus, she serves the Specialty by
> candlelight, with the wine which the beau brings.
>
> After a few unadmitted failures, however, she
> gives up the Specialty and settles for spaghetti
> flooded with "her" great sauce, which she makes
> from hamburger meat, canned tomatoes, and too
> much oregano....

Among upper-middles there's a general belief that sliced
bread is, *ipso facto*, horrible, although some allowance
may be made for brands pleading a degree of archaism, like Arnold's Brick Oven or Pepperidge "Farm."
Abroad is the magic notion here. Sometimes it seems
that anything will be consumed so long as it's not na-
tive. Thus the parade of pâtés, unpasteurized cheese
and wine, morels, escargots, pasta, and moussaka. But
some lines are drawn: tacos and pizza are out, and so
are common "Chinese" dishes. At the moment Japa-
nese is in, Chinese (except for "Setzuan") rather out,
and Mexican irredeemably vulgar. Light white wine or
beer is drunk with these things.

Down in the middle and prole worlds, on the other
hand, the thing to drink with the evening meal is likely
to be either some sort of "soda," like Coca-Cola or
ginger ale, "black raspberry" or "creme," or, among
proles, beer, almost always in the can. The middle-
class fear of ideology we noticed in their home décor
has its counterpart in their flight from sharp flavors in

food. This is where meals are fashioned out of the bland and the soft and the blah, and where the very mention of garlic causes the eyeballs to roll back. Even onions are used sparingly, and canned fruits (or fruit cocktail) are preferred to the real thing both because they are sweeter and because they are more tasteless. Purveyors of food to the middle class have learned from disillusioning but profitable experience that to designate anything MILD (like cheese or mustard) is to increase volume, while to say nothing or go so far as to label it STRONG or SPICY is risky. Spicy effects return near the bottom of the status ladder, where "ethnic" items begin to appear: Polish sausage, hot pickles, and the like. This is the main reason the middle class abjures such tastes, believing them associated with low people, non-Anglo-Saxon foreigners, recent immigrants, and such riffraff, who can almost always be identified by their fondness for unambiguous and ungenteel flavors. Soon there will be a whole generation, sprung from middle-class loins and feeding largely out of freezers, which will assume that "fish" is white mushy stuff, very like "bread," and will turn to horse, coke, pot, hash, or Seagram's and Seven as more interesting.

Ice cream, at once both sweet and soft, is the favorite middle-class treat. And the very kind of ice cream you like has class meaning. Vanilla is at the top, with chocolate considerably below. Strawberry and other fruit flavors are near the bottom. In gauging the class of Edward Koch, the New York politician, you don't have to know much more than that his favorite ice-cream flavors are chocolate and butter almond. When Arthur Penn, maker of the film *Bonnie and Clyde*, wanted to stigmatize that gang as a bunch of bad proles, he had them "send out" for *peach* ice cream. You can imagine the whole embarrassing class situation presupposed by Carvel's Ice Cream Cakes.

If ice cream is a vivid class indicator, so, of course, is the kind of place where you buy it and your other foodstuffs. In fact, in the suburban town I live in there's hardly a clearer class indicator. The uppers and some of the upper-middles phone their orders in and have things delivered by a nice man who says good morning and puts the perishables away in your refrigerator. Ten years ago there were six such small markets that delivered. Now there is one. (See the material on Prole Drift in Chapter VIII.) The lesser upper-middles and the middles hump their own stuff home from the A&P. The proles shop at the Acme or the Food Fair, distinguished from the A&P by slightly lower prices, a lesser grade of meat, and, most important, the absence on the shelves of anything exotic or frightening, or even "foreign." One reason top people like to give phone orders for food is that they like being bossy, and it's fun also to show off by pronouncing properly the names of imported items like uncommon cheeses.

Let us move to "eating out." A fixation with both middles and proles, since it gives you a chance to play King and Queen for a Day, issuing orders, being waited on, affecting to be somebody. And by frequenting a restaurant said to put out "gourmet" food—pronounced *goor-máy*—the middle class can play the game it loves most, pretending to be in the class above, in restaurants especially inviting observers to identify it with traveled upper-middle-class people presumably of delicate and sophisticated tastes. In a gourmet restaurant you can use your own little silver pepper mill ("for the traveling gourmet"), which you got for Christmas and carry in a fleecy little pouch. The establishment aiming to capture a middle-class clientele will go in for a lot of *flambé* and accompany it with plenty of piped music of the blander sort—lots of strings. A woman

executive secretary, a high-school graduate, told Studs
Terkel: "I have dinner with businessmen and enjoy this
very much. I like the background music in some of
these restaurants. It's soothing and it also adds a little
warmth and doesn't disturb the conversation. I like the
atmosphere and the caliber of people that usually you
see and run into. People who have made it."

There it is in a horrible little nutshell. What makes
that comment middle-class is that it never touches on
the food, middle-class clients being drawn to restaurants largely by the arts of the decorator and the orchestra leader rather than the skill of the chef. Near
where I live there's a restaurant which in no way both-
ers to conceal its much greater pride in the décor than
in the cuisine. Its various dining rooms are done in
every conceivable fake historical style, like colonial,
Victorian, and Tudor; and a sign in each room calls
diners' attention to such "authentic" details as carpets,
wallpaper, and furniture. One room offers a "jungle"
setting with trees and exotic flora and a waterfall spill-
ing into a pool with moss-covered banks—"a Tarzan
movie set," a critic has observed, "complete with dangling vines." In such places the food will be the customary frozen schlock, soft, tasteless, and impressively
expensive, prefabricated dishes warmed in a battery
of microwave ovens not by chefs but by a squad of
heating engineers. Because the middle class believes
its betters go in for "elegance," this concept makes
conspicuous appearances in advertising designed to
drag them in:

Élégance Par Excellence
The elegant new Mon Rêve Restaurant brings distinguished dining to Indianapolis. Classic French
cuisine which meets an international standard of
perfection. Impeccable service. In a shimmering

setting of silk, Strauss crystal and silver. An experienced staff from the fine restaurants of Europe,
New York, Chicago and Cincinnati.

That whole performance, despite the way the final sentence illustrates the art of sinking in prose, suggests
the appeal of the handbill advertising The Royal None-
such in *Huckleberry Finn*. As the Duke says of the
stipulation LADIES AND CHILDREN NOT ADMITTED, "If
that line don't fetch them, I don't know Arkansaw."
The "Mon Rêve" is clearly the sort of fake-elegant
restaurant where the diner is not allowed to pour his
own wine but must drink at the sufferance of the waiter,
who hovers mock-solicitously, now and then, but never
at the right time, filling the glass to the very brim. In
the Southwest, rather near the Mexican border, that
sort of restaurant will offer *Filet* (or sometimes *Fillet*)
Miñon. Sometimes, resisting for a change the appeal
of restaurants like that, the middle class will frequent
"dinner theater," a way of positively guaranteeing that
both food and theater will be amateur and mediocre,
which means unthreatening and therefore desirable.

The prole restaurant, on the other hand, will at least
be unpretentious. No *flambé* there, no fraudulent
French accents or flagrant misspellings of the French
on the menu. The help in such places are really just
folks, like you, and you get into long, intensely friendly
conversations with them. "How's your mother's scia-
tica, dear?" On both sides there's a strong desire to
be liked, rather than admired, and an ambition not by
any means to be thought hoity-toity. Like prole meals
at home, eating out at a prole restaurant means doing
it early and fast. In minor cities in the Middle West
your average high-prole businessman's lunch is over
well before 1:30. After that, restaurants are deserted
and the staff begins setting the tables for dinner, which

will seldom take place later than 6:00. In restaurants, proles never risk the unknown on the menu, which means they tend to feed on dishes familiar in Army messes or college dining facilities, things like meat loaf, liver and onions (sometimes "and bacon strip"), "Swiss" steak, fish on Friday, and macaroni and cheese. All these are flaccid, having been kept some time in the handy steam table. In the higher kind of prole restaurant the stainless-steel cutlery will be cast instead of stamped out and there will be a salad bar offering iceberg lettuce and a variety of cut-up vegetables, all frigid and tasting alike. In these places very weak coffee, permitting you to see all the way to the bottom of the cup when it's filled, will be served with the main course.

Television advertising presents a telling picture of prole eating habits. Not so much the ads for the foods themselves, but the ads for what follows, the "antacids" like Tums, Rolaids, Di-Gel, and Alka Seltzer. The immense local traffic in such commodities seems uniquely American: at least I've never seen its equivalent in Britain, France, Italy, or Germany. Only we seem to have developed a multibillion-dollar industry based on proles' eating junk (consider the chili hot dog, for example) and then taking junk—chalk, largely— to overcome the effects of eating it. And you can infer the popularity among proles of eating *breakfast* out by a TV ad for a brand of doughnuts (speaking of the need for antacids) that exhorts Mom to "Keep 'Em Home for Breakfast." One gathers that the tasteless sausage patty eaten out is preferable to the fairly nice one you can fry up at home. For an explanation, I think we could go to the Veblen who analyzes conspicuous expenditure in public. But the difference now is that it's less the upper than the lower orders who, to fulfill their fantasies, are moved to exhibit their purchasing power, even early in the morning when the audience is minimal

and bound to consist largely of other proles responding
to the same ad.

Before moving on from the topic of drinking and
eating in relation to television, we should pause to
consider the class meaning of a traditional social event
held in January. I refer to the Super Bowl party, a
fixture found among the middle class, to be sure, but
which comes wholly into its own among proles. But
not the lowest proles, for they never "entertain" or
have people in (except relatives). These Super Bowl
parties are often Bring Your Own Bottle affairs, but
sometimes they are a copious and expensive bash paid
for entirely by the host to show his power and desirability. His wife will provide an elaborate buffet, and
he will supply the beer and sometimes even the bourbon and ginger, and often he will rent, for around four
hundred dollars, a projecting TV set with a large movie
screen so that all can see the action. In some prole com-
munities "Super Sunday" is regarded as the biggest day
of the year, and to ridicule it would be to risk corporal
rebuke. The satiric anti-Super Bowl party is sometimes
heard of, in New York and similar skeptical, un-American places. Here the whole occasion is set up by keeping the TV set dark during game time while the guests
drink vodka and talk of anything but sports.

Thus drink and food adhesions, which broadcast
your class position with very little ambiguity. So do
your practices in "weekending," "summering," and
"traveling," as well as your preferences in sports, both
do-it-yourself and spectating. As a class concept, the
"weekend" has suffered a sad comedown and proletarianization in the last hundred years. The term dates
only from 1878, a moment marking what can be said
to be the flowering of high bourgeois culture. Then,
"weekend" could connote overnight stays at splendid

houses in the country. Then, the weekend houseguest could stand in need of advice like this, still available in the British *Debrett's Etiquette and Modern Manners* (1981): "If you are going to stay at a rather grand house that is fully staffed, it is worth bearing in mind when packing that your suitcase may be *unpacked* by someone else." (That is, omit embarrassing sexual accessories.) From that sort of grandeur, aped once by the upper and upper-middle classes here, the concept "weekend" has taken on largely middle-class or high-prole associations, betokening now the momentary freedom custom and the law oblige employers to grant their wage slaves. That the weekend is now widely regarded as a mere prole entertainment fixture is clear from the vulgar "Weekend" sections of papers like the *New York Times* and the *San Francisco Chronicle*, brimming over with commercial features and ads telling the presumably witless consumers what to do. Formerly those who weekended seemed to know how to spend their time without needing to be instructed by merchandisers and journalists. From the moment in the 1950s when a cheap brand of cigarette called *Weekend* began appearing in France, it was clear that as a stylish idea, *weekend* was done for. It should hardly be necessary to indicate that for uppers, who do not have employers or perform steady work, the weekend is not a very meaningful concept, except as it indicates the days when the banks are closed.

If *weekend* is essentially a prole, because an employee's, notion, *summering* is upper-middle-class and higher. As Lisa Birnbach and her acute colleagues note, "The summer is the high point of the Prep year..., the point of reference for everything else in life. You choose your clothing, car, friends, pets, on the basis of where and how you summer. The Jeep because you summer on rough terrain. The sailboat motif because you sail during the summer." Not that proles don't summer too, in their way, but their way is seldom to summer every year in the same place, and the place is unlikely not just to be owned by them but to have been in the family for several generations. Prole "summer" is never three months long, but two weeks, or at most, four. They summer at an attraction specially built for them, like the Disney fun parks, which they will, in a sense, "rent" while there and then relinquish. On the prole principle that the public knows what's best, the prole will always go where others go, preferably to stand in line once he's there.

As I've indicated elsewhere, in our day, travel has been reduced so entirely to tourism that one can hardly use the archaic and honorific term anymore except ironically. So I'll call the activity tourism. All classes are its victims, but proles least of all, not so much because they can't afford it as because they fear the new experiences they imagine it might offer. The wholly predictable is what they want, not the unexpected, and the irony is that the wholly predictable is exactly what tourism now provides. But proles are still slightly scared even of tourism. As Arthur B. Shostak says of proles in *Blue-Collar Life* (1969), they tend to choose experiences for their leisure "that have the power *to affirm acquired wisdom* rather than provide any confrontations with novel and possibly taxing matters." The strange can be very threatening to proles, and tourism, they think, offers numerous menaces: "One must relate to strangers, adroitly step in and out of roles, and competently meet unexpected developments.... Fears of 'being taken'... combine... with provincial ignorance of where one might go, smugness in concluding little elsewhere is really worth visiting, and preference for the hometown version of things." These fears tend to limit prole trips to visits with relatives or drives to relatives' funerals. When they do take a trip, they remember it for years and dwell on its details of meals, mileages, expenses, and motel luxuries ("They even had a strip of paper across the toilet seat").

The touristic class is predominantly the middle, the one that has made Hawaii, as Roger Price unkindly designates it, "Roob Valhalla." The middle is the class that makes cruise ships a profitable enterprise, for it fancies that the upper-middle class is to be mixed with on them, without realizing that that class is either peering at the minarets in Istanbul, or hiding out in a valley in Nepal, or staying home in Old Lyme, Connecticut, playing backgammon and reading *Town and Country*. Tourism is popular with the middle class because it allows them to "*buy* the feeling," as C. Wright Mills says, "if only for a short time, of higher status." And as he points out, both cruise (or resort) staffs and their clientele cooperate in playing out the charade that really quite an upper-middle-class (or even upper-class) operation is going forward: lots of "served meals," white napery, "sparkling wine," mock caviar. If you'll notice how often, in tourist advertising, the term *luxury* appears (as well as the word *gourmet*), you'll see what I mean. For what the middle class most envies in the classes above is their trips abroad, more than their houses, cars, or other items of local conspicuous consumption. And, as Richard P. Coleman and Lee Rainwater perceive in their book *Social Standing in America* (1978), the envy is more than economic—it's "cultural": "Cultural superiority is symbolized" by the uppers' experiences of distant places, and the uppers' habit of tripping "seems to say that the traveler is already comfortable in such settings or is in the process of becoming so."

WINTER BEDROOM OF AN UPPER-MIDDLE-CLASS YOUNG
PERSON

The upper class usually tours independently, without joining a group: quite natural, for in any group there
would surely be some people one wouldn't care to
know. The one exception is going on an "art tour" with
certified equals, often organized by one's college and
accompanied not by guides but by "lecturers" and "art
historians." Of course one's presence on such a tour
underlines one's ignorance, intellectual laziness, and
lack of curiosity just as firmly as if one were on a
normal vulgar "guided tour," but class accrues because
one is looking at art and at the same time borrowing

some of the prestige associated with the choicer institutions of higher learning.

Class accrues also, of course, from participation and even interest in sports. But not all sports, only certain carefully selected ones. A prole aspiring to rise can ascertain what the right ones are by simply entering a good men's shop—that is, an upper-middle-class one— and scrutinizing the neckties which John T. Molloy advises him to invest in. From these he'll learn as much about the OK-ness of certain sports as from the sports themselves. He'll notice ties depicting, as Molloy says, "a little fish with a fly in its mouth, a tennis racquet, a sailboat, a golf ball or club, a horse or polo bat, etc." But there are class pitfalls even here. One must learn that fishing in fresh water is classier than in salt, and that if salmon and trout are the things to catch, a catfish is something by all means to avoid catching. Salmon fishing is classy, of course, because associated with Scotland. The same principle makes curling a class sport. (Bocce, being Mediterranean, as well as sending out slight Mafia signals, is prole.) Tennis has suffered a bit in class since the proliferation of free municipal courts, but still, at its best, it requires a handsome and expensive costume, equipment, and "lessons" and thus qualifies as an upper-middle-class enterprise at least. Knowing how to sail a boat well is so indispensable to upper-middle-class status that it can almost serve as a class division in itself. And of course racing a boat is higher than just tooling about in one. Golf is slipping a bit now as a high-status sport: today you can even overhear high proles discussing their games. But it still generally fulfills the requirements set down by Alison Lurie:

A high-status sport, by definition, is one that requires a great deal of expensive equipment or an

expensive setting or both; ideally, it will use up
goods and services rapidly. Golf, for instance, demands the withdrawal from cultivation, housing or
commercial use of many acres of valuable land; the
resulting golf course must be constantly weeded,
watered, mown and rolled with high-cost machines.

True enough. And a perfect example of Lurie's high-
class sport that uses up goods and services rapidly is
skeet shooting, where a successful session is measured
precisely by how many clay discs have Gone West.
Although skiing has now sunk to middle-class status
and even below, it began as a class sport because it
was expensive, inconvenient, and practiced only in
distant places. And dangerous, which meant that it was
one of the sources, like today's snowmobiles and
mopeds, of the white badge of honor—the plaster cast
on leg or ankle worn during the winter by members of
the three top classes. This white badge signifies a high
degree of conspicuous waste in a social world where
questions of unpayable medical bills or missed working
days do not apply. One can also earn the white badge
from mishaps with horses. Riding is a class sport not
just because, like yachting, it's expensive, but because
it's so archaic. It also permits you to look down on
people. Lisa Birnbach has come up with a fairly sound
formula for estimating the class of games played in
school and college: the balls used in top-class games
are generally smaller than those used in the others.
Thus the superiority of golf, tennis, and squash to football, basketball, volleyball, and baseball. And of course
bowling.

Because it's the most expensive, yachting beats all
other recreations as a theater for upper-status exhibition. But certain inviolable principles apply. Sail is
still far superior to power, partly because you can't do

it simply by turning an ignition key and steering—you have to be sort of to the manner born. (Probably the most vulgar vessel you can own is a Chris-Craft, the yachting equivalent of the Mercedes.) The yacht must be quite long, at least thirty-five feet, and in getting a new one you must constantly trade up, never down. According to one yacht broker, boat status proceeds by five-foot increments. The customers, he says, will "jump up five feet at a time until they get up to sixty or seventy feet." And the yacht should aim at the uncomfortable racing style rather than the dumpy, folksy, family style, which might suggest living on it all the time, thus hinting at privation. For this reason houseboats are at the class bottom, like trailers, failing on at least three counts: if movable, they're moved by power, not sail; they're comfortable boats with lots of room; and one lives on them. In smaller racing yachts of the higher classes, archaism and internationalism figure. Because they're old and unlocal, the Star and the six-meter have lots of status.

In the matter of the material yacht hulls are made of you can see the two essential principles which confer class on objects, organicism and archaism, operating together as they do so often. Boats made of wood are classier than boats made of the cheaper and more practical fiberglass: the stuff they are made of was once alive, and when boats are made of it they have the status of virtual antiques, like Oriental rugs. And when repairs or replacements are necessary, they're more expensive. For yachtsmen who appreciate the snob value of wooden hulls, there's even a magazine, *Wooden Boat*, published in Brooklyn, Maine, which reminds them regularly of the cause of their superiority.

Among indoor games, bridge and of course backgammon are quite high. Scrabble is middle-class, like canasta. Chess is seldom found above the upper-middle class: it's too hard. Billiards has status only if a separate room, rather large, is devoted to it exclusively. Billiard tables which, once a cover is set into place, become the family dining table are high-prole. So are billiard tables any smaller than the largest size.

If the upper orders have yachts, what do proles have? Bowling. If you want to maintain upper status, it's important that you never, never go bowling. Taking it up can instantly declass an upper-middle-class per-

BALLS, HIGH AND LOW

son. Bowling is popular with proles for many reasons. For one thing, you can drink and smoke while doing it. For another, if you get on a company team, you wear a nifty uniform shirt made of satin with your own name machine-embroidered in script above one pocket. Another attraction is that it's one sport you don't have to strip down to play: you can be good at it and still keep your prole fatty tissue decently covered. Over the years there's been some attempt to raise the social status of bowling by euphemism and genteelism: what used to be called *alleys* are now *lanes*, and *gutters* are now *channels*. But to no avail. Bowling remains the classic prole sport, and proles can't get too much of it: those who buy a Bowler's Prayer plaque at their local religious-goods store can be found on Saturday afternoon settled comfortably in front of the TV with plenty of canned Miller's in the refrigerator, studying every move on *Bowling for Dollars*.

Which brings up the matter of the class meaning of sports fanship and spectatorhood. Short of watching such Anglophile exercises as cricket and polo, hard to do in this country, the most class probably attaches to watching tennis, even at the newly proletarianized— that is, modernized—Forest Hills. Watching golf is good too, and so is watching the Americas Cup race at Newport, Rhode Island. Watching them all "live" is of course better than watching them on TV because it takes conspicuous expenditure to get there. On television, below golf comes baseball, and below that, football. Then ice hockey. Then boxing, stock-car racing, bowling, and, at the bottom, Roller Derby, once popular with advertisers until they discovered that the people watching it were so low-prole or even destitute that they constituted an entirely wasted audience for the commercials: they couldn't buy anything at all, not even detergents, antacids, and beer. "Low-Reach Undesirables," the Roller Derby audience became known in the trade, and the event that had attracted them was soon removed from television.

Two motives urge middle-class and prole fans to obsession with their sports. One is their need as losers to identify with winners, the need to dance and scream "We're number one!" while holding an index finger erect. One hockey player says: "The whole object of a pro game is to win. That is what we sell. We sell it to a lot of people who don't win at all in their regular lives. They involve themselves with *their* team, a winning team." In addition to this appeal through vicarious success, sports are popular for middles and proles to follow because they sanction a flux of pedantry, dogmatism, record-keeping, wise secret knowledge, and pseudo-scholarship of the sort usually associated with the "decision-making" or "executive" or "opinion-molding" classes. The World Series and the Super Bowl give every man his opportunity to perform as a learned bore, to play for the moment the impressive barroom pedant, to imitate for a brief season the superior classes identified by their practice of weighty utterance and informed opinion. Which is to say that the World Series and the Super Bowl constitute harmless twice-yearly opportunities—occurring, oddly, near the winter and summer solstices, as if designed by Nature herself—for the plain man to garner some self-respect. They are therefore indispensable as democratic holy days and ritual occasions. If the prole doesn't know what might cause Union Carbide to go up or down, as a master of "the fine points of the game" he can affect to know why the Chargers or the Dodgers are going to win this time, and that's a powerful need satisfied. The barroom or living-room debates occasioned by these events are a prole counterpart of the classy debates in statehouses and courthouses, and the shrewd weighing of evidence and thoughtful drawing of inferences ape the proceedings in the highest learned conferences and seminars. In addition, the satire and abuse visited upon holders of opposite views, especially in bars, is the prole equivalent of the contumely dispensed by the better book reviewers and theater critics.

Exercising authority in learned matters like these is one way the middle and prole classes assert their value. Another way is buying things, especially from mail-order catalogs. Addressed to "Resident," these tumble through the mail slot all year long but most profusely about three months before national holidays associated with "gifting." Despite their occasional complaints

CLASS FANTASIZING BY MEANS OF THE CATALOG

about junk mail, Resident secretly likes receiving these catalogs, for they suggest that someone out there believes he has money and recognizes that he has the power to choose. Middles and proles like these catalogs too because if you buy from them instead of from a store you don't risk being humiliated by some snotty clerk, and no one, not even the postman, knows what you're buying. Catalog buying is the perfect way for the insecure and the hypersensitive and the socially uncertain to sustain their selfhood by accumulating goods. The things bought are not important things—indeed, almost everything offered in these catalogs is conspicuously unnecessary, except as a device to sustain the ego. King Lear, in saying, "O reason not the need," would recognize what's going on here, and so, probably, would De Tocqueville, who wrote in 1845 after taking a long, hard look at the American scene: "Among democratic nations, ambition is ardent and continual, but its aim is not habitually lofty; and life is generally spent in eagerly coveting small objects that are within reach." He means *goals*, of course, but his formulation works just as well if you think of chrome-plated ice tongs, Hummel figurines, and imitation silver bookmarks reading "Dan Burris: His Book."

The middle class is the main clientele for these catalogs, and the things they buy from them assure them of their value and support their aspirations. When the music-box lid is opened, one is regaled by "The Impossible Dream," suggesting that wishing may make it so, that if you're a good boy you can get an invitation to summer with the upper-middle class on Mackinac Island or achieve admission to the Yale School of Law. The way some items are advertised suggests that the purchaser is already well on his way to upper-middle-class status, where one finds the "discriminating people" and the "people of refinement." Thus the invitation to invest in "Six very individual hand-blown crystal liqueur glasses to serve your carefully selected cordials." "Gold" things—tableware, cutlery—seem much in demand: they wouldn't fool anyone, of course, but then they just might. King Lear would have little trouble understanding the appeal of gold-plated dice "in a suede cloth pouch." You can advertise your one-time association with a class institution by ordering a needlepoint canvas imprinted with "your alma mater's seal." Touchingly, the one in the illustration is not the University of Delaware, but Harvard.

For the middle class with upward longings, the great class totem is "Mother England," as one catalog puts it ("These are some of the [regimental-striped] ties that bind us to Mother England"). Many catalogs get down to the Anglophilic job right at the beginning by displaying the Union Jack on the cover. One announces, "We are unabashedly Anglophiles" and then goes on to associate Britain with strictly organic materials like wool and leather. From this company you can buy a cavalry saber and a "matching" copy of Churchill's *My Early Life* ($17.50). Another catalog sells Anglophilic bookmarks in silver, fashioned into portraits of three great Britons—Shakespeare, Churchill, and Sherlock Holmes. Apparently no item is so ugly and preposterous that it won't go if given a pseudo-British name, like an unfortunate combined candle snuffer and candle holder cast in brass. If it were called "The Hackensack, New Jersey, Candle Tool," it would surely not succeed. It is called "The Kensington Candle Snuffer" and described as "A mantle [*sic*] accessory that will add a touch of gracious English charm to your home." Likewise, there's a mock-silver bread server advertised as "From the Court of King George." Yes, but which one? I, II, III, IV, V, or VI? No matter—*King* is the operative word. (Perhaps it will come as no surprise that one of the most snobbish mail-order houses purveying British goods is located in Tempe, Arizona.)

Catalogs aimed at the middle class seem to assume that only clients imagining themselves "British" in descent constitute an audience for "heraldic" items ("Is Your [Anglo-Saxon] Name Here? Your Family's Coat-of-Arms Beautifully Embossed on Imitation Parchment"). No sort of hustle is apparently too coarse to work with the middle class, so deep is its need for a reputable (that is, British) family background. One catalog, for example, offers a set of twenty-four drinking glasses "emblazoned" (I am quoting) with "your own family name and coat of arms." And then in tiny type:

> The Sanson Institute of Heraldry will select from our records and reference books the coat of arms shown to have been borne at some time in the past by a person of your surname or an onomatological variant. No genealogical relationship between your family and the persons who originally bore the coat of arms selected is intended or implied.

The audience for this hoax is suggested, sadly, by the accompanying credit information indicating that you can get these glasses and attendant documentation for "Only $5.99 per month for 10 months, plus applicable finance charges." Similarly, Scots who feel that a loss of status attended their family's immigration to this country are catered to by catalogs selling them goods conferring archaistic self-esteem, like "clan" wall plaques and numerous items made from "your" tartan, such as anomalous "Tartan neckties." Also those little Scottish men's tams that make anyone wearing one south of the Tweed look an absolute fool. All these "heraldic" and "clan" appurtenances register the depth and pathos of the feeling of unimportance which is the bugbear and stigma of the middle class. "They feel that they live in a time of big decisions," says C. Wright Mills, but "they know that they are not making any." Thus the existence in the United States of an organization called "Americans of Royal Descent": Twain's Duke and Dauphin, we realize, are entirely in the American grain.

One way the catalogs recognize the middle class's need to argue its deep if not potentially archaic roots is to offer it the opportunity to accumulate valuable "collections" to pass on as heirlooms to future generations. The imagery implies that every man is his own Huntington or Frick or Morgan, beginning a bit late, to be sure, but at least starting to gather a collection certain to have investment as well as familial value. The appeal to greed here is obvious: "Increasingly hard-to-find Victorian toast racks are good investments for collectors." In fact, peddling "collector's items" to the middle and lower classes has now reached a fine art. Witness the Norman Rockwell plate sold for $20, with suggestions that it will increase in value (!), having been produced in a "limited edition" during only "one hundred firing days"; in that time, obviously, billions of the hideous things can be turned out. What distinguishes all these catalog "collectibles" is that they are at once ugly, of doubtful value, and expensive—mass-produced Beatrix Potter character figurines at $15.50 each; porcelain Hummel figures at $42; Anglophilic Toby jugs at $52.50; and the quintessential emblems of Anglophilia, Royal Doulton figurines ("our price, $122.50"). Nothing is too ugly or valueless to be offered by the catalogs as an item to be "collected" so long as it is priced high enough. One middle-class catalog features a set of six "Collector Wine Glasses" of a really extraordinary lack of distinction, their stems consisting of little porcelain figures of a man, a woman, a priest, and the like, and their glass rims gilded. They

are absolutely awful, and six of them, bought by in-
nocents for "investment" purposes, cost $125.

   Imagine yourself an upper-middle-class visitor being
shown around a middle-class "home." It all looks very
nice, very clean and neat, etc. But one thing's puzzling:
against a wall there's a tall, shallow display case made
of walnut veneer with scores of long shelves protected
from the world by a transparent acrylic "glass" front.
You've never seen anything like it, and it gets even
more puzzling the closer you inspect what it's displaying: hundred of "novelty thimbles" crowded side
by side in long ranks.
   "What's that?" you ask.
   "That's my thimble collection."
   "Your what?"
   "My thimble collection."
   "Ummm. Where do you—ahem—get them all?"
   "From catalogs."
   "Where?"
   "Mail-order catalogs."
You are kind enough not to ask, "Why?" for they
are a study: there's a "gavel thimble," a royal-wedding
thimble, and a "Pope's Miter Thimble: tiny bisque rep-
lica of miter worn by Pope John Paul II when celebrating mass in U.S. in 1979"; there are porcelain
thimbles with pastoral scenes and improving texts, and
there's a thimble with an appliqué gold-plated actual
leaf from the actual "Vienna Woods." You realize with
a start that this country must be swarming with middle-
class novelty-thimble collectors. And this sweet lady
who's showing you her collection thinks not merely
that it's interesting; she thinks it's valuable, and that's
the awful thing.
   I feel very sorry for this woman. Her presence is
implied everywhere in these middle-class catalogs, es-

pecially when they offer items associated with kitchen work. One such is a plaque designed to be hung up by the housewife who suspects that she's really only a sorry drudge. By exhibiting these verses, she can raise her spirits and also attract consolatory, if not congratulatory, notice from others:

> Bless the kitchen in which I cook.
> Bless each moment within this nook.
> Let joy and laughter share this room
> With spices, skillet, and my broom.
> Bless me and mine with love and health
> And I'll not ask for greater wealth.

(Personally, I find notable pathos in the third and fourth lines, which specify, as if lovingly, the implements of the speaker's slavery.) A plaque like that, designed to represent a misfortune as an advantage, has its counterpart in the "Irish Tote" one catalog offers. This canvas carrying bag reads, in green lettering with attendant shamrocks, "'Tis a Blessing to be IRISH." The rhetorical technique—unlikely insistence, we can call it—is similar to the one in the ad slogan "I Love New York."

Some of the items offered the middle class in these catalogs wryly recognize the purchasers' pathetic psychic requirements, like a four-inch-high brass cymbal mounted on a wooden stand: inch-high block letters read STATUS CYMBAL. Similar is the pillow (costing $25) which presents the message

> NOUVEAU RICHE
> IS BETTER THAN
> NO RICHE AT ALL.

Practically all that need be known about the psychological circumstances of the middle class is latent in the "Champagne Recork" which Hammacher Schlemmer purveys. "This unusual stopper," the catalog indicates, "keeps 'bubbly' sprightly, sparkling after uncorking ceremony is over. Gold electro-plated." There you have it: at once the desire for grandeur and the need for prudence, the two contradictory motives at perpetual war in the hearts of those caught in the middle.

On the other hand, the hearts of the top classes would seem, on the evidence of the catalogs directed to them, largely free of this sort of internal warfare, at least. The upper-middle-class audience for catalogs issued by the Talbots and L.L. Bean and "The Horchow Collection" (Dallas) knows what it wants in its *bibelots*; expensive throwaways, largely things to give people who already have everything. From these upper catalogs you can order a silver ice-cream-cone holder, silver candle snuffers, trick corkscrews, gold or silver collar stays (honorific because clearly useless to the recipient, who always wears Oxford-cloth button-downs), sets of small solid-brass cowboy boots for tamping out cigarette butts in ashtrays, heating sets for brandy snifters made of brass tubing and little alcohol lamps. There's no question here of anyone's buying this stuff to sustain either ego or aspiration, for up here ego is secure and aspiration unknown.

How can you tell if a catalog is either upper-middle-class or upper-class? For one thing, whenever a color photo depicts a bread basket or a bread warmer, it will be filled not with rolls or muffins or similar plebeian breadstuffs but with croissants. Again, these catalogs offer a disproportionate number of Chinese artifacts (like "ginger jars"), betokening as they do a close connection with the "old" Orient, the archaic one Americans used to colonize, missionary to, educate, patronize, and rip off. You may also infer that a catalog is upper-class if it sells a life-size metal suit of armor—complete with sword—for $2,450: "All joints are fully moveable, as is the visor." You can either display the

suit on a stand or, even though the ensemble weighs
seventy-five pounds, wear it to a party and introduce
drinks into the helmet through the visor.

But the main indication that a catalog is upper-class
is that it sells clothes. If something doesn't fit or look
right when it arrives, for the rich no matter—give it
away, either to the Salvation Army or to the servants.
Proles can't afford such risks in their consuming. Even
when they do buy clothes from their prole catalogs,
and risk is small because the clothes are not sized, as
in the His and Her Slumber Suits made of T-shirt cot-
ton-knit printed with the combat camouflage pattern
(why? why on earth?) or the similar matched night-
shirts (red, or red-and-white striped) reading on the
pocket, "Brr, I'm Cold."

If the middle class buys for its morale and the upper
for laughs, proles buy to pay their respects to technology and art. Space-scientific electronic watches (with
musical alarms) are popular, and so, of course, are
cameras, the more complex the better, and stereos and
color TVs, ditto. No pocket computer is too pretentious to be flogged by mail to proles. And then there
are the artistic items: a porcelain egg with Nativity
scene in bas relief; a "musical gondola..., beautifully
designed in elaborately embossed brass. Gondola re-
volves on pedestal base to 'O Sole Mio.' Hinged treasure box opens to reveal elegant red velvet interior."
Also dark glasses with lenses in the shape of hearts;
an acrylic-pile wall hanging the size of a blanket depicting a stallion running toward the viewer; a horse-
stall photo-door (a mural you can paste up on a wall),
showing a horse looking out over a stall door (every
house a stable); "Your pet hand-painted on needlepoint
canvas: send us a good color photograph"; license-
plate frames reading (again) "Happiness is being a
grandparent." And a dinner plate with a color photo

of your dog on it ("You'll treasure [it] for years to come.... Add $4.50 for personalization up to 25 letters"). Some prole items are not artistic but clever and labor-saving, like the classic nose-hair clippers. And some are sentimental and "traditional," like the toilet roll with "Merry Christmas" printed on each sheet in Old English type ("Makes a wonderful little gift"). One thing notable about current prole catalogs is the virtual disappearance of novelty banks, the kind that, before inflation made "saving" a cruel joke, you used to insert coins into, to save for your education or for taking a wonderful trip someday.

One surefire prole stigma in catalogs is the Christian emphasis. One exemplar bills itself as "A Christian Family Catalog," which prepares the reader to encounter scores of self-congratulatory mottos on little mock-wooden plaques, things like "Lord, help me to remember that nothing is going to happen to me today that You and I together can't handle," or "When you help someone up a steep hill you get nearer the top yourself," or "You have touched me; I have grown." If the function of the middle-class housewife's plaque is to assure her that her drudgery has value, the function of these plaques is to assert that God loves proles, which He doubtless does, although there seems no reason for constantly harping on it.

One feature of prole catalogs is the frequency with which the unicorn, of all things, appears. We find plush unicorns, pewter unicorns, brass unicorns, "Porcelain Revolving Musical Unicorns"—every conceivable avatar of unicorn. As one catalog announces, "Unicorns are all the rage these days." I've spent six months trying to find out exactly why, and I'm finally stumped. Perhaps the reason is a highly selective if low Anglophilic snobbery which has abstracted the unicorn from the British royal arms, for some reason leaving behind the lion, a much classier animal, one would think. Perhaps the popularity of Tolkien (but not among proles, surely?) has stimulated interest in "mythical animals," any and all of them. Perhaps it's the exoticism (and presumed rarity, and thus value) of the unicorn that stimulates the prole fancy. It may be important that the unicorn, unlike the dragon, is one mythical animal which is wholly benign, thus resembling such real creatures singled out for canonization by proles as whales, dolphins, pandas, and koala bears. And for learned proles, the unicorn may be vaguely associated with sex—there's the dimly recalled connection with virgins, the phallicism of the horn, etc. Whatever the reason for the unicorn's popularity among proles, the motif is an example of what literary critics used to denigrate as *pseudo-reference*. The thing seems to refer, portentously, to something more specific than it does. I have before me a pretentious prole drawing which comes on as loaded with meaning. It shows a unicorn bursting fully formed out of an egg (!) against a rainbow and a vaguely "zodiacal" star-studded sky. The animal is himself (herself?) also dotted with stars. Meaning? Well, there isn't any, as a matter of fact, but there seems to be, and that's a prole sufficiency, gratifying the dual desire for the portentous and the vague.

Proles join with the middle class in the pleasure with which they contemplate their own names, which is to say, the assurance they derive from knowing that they are not as anonymous and replaceable as society, in its dealings with them, seems to imply. Hence the popularity among both these classes of having their catalog purchases "personalized." This need is like that of little children who by similar means gain assurance of their identity and value: "This is my very own shoe bag," "My very own cup and plate," etc. Thus from one

CORNER OF A HIGH-PROLE LIVING ROOM AFTER DEEP
INVESTMENT IN THE MOTIF OF THE PERIOD

middle-class catalog you can order His-Her wrist-
watches, with "John" on the face of one, "Mary" on
the other. This feature will bring you pleasure countless times a day as you glance at your wrist to ascertain
the time and find your own valuable name there: what
a comfort—you are somebody after all. The motive is
recognizably similar to the one impelling the destitute
delinquents who deface subway cars to do so with
graffiti consisting of the artist's name and address.
The psychic predicament of users of flagrantly mass-
produced articles can be inferred from the prole and
middle-class need to buy from their catalogs a little
mock-brass plate you stick onto the dashboard of your
car.
It reads

CUSTOM BUILT FOR [NAME]

The full meaning of that little plate would be understood by the Walt Whitman intensely aware of threats to the self posed by the American emphasis on the *en masse*.

There's hardly anything you get from a catalog that can't be personalized. You can get a Lucite napkin ring, personalized with three initials; you can get a canvas log carrier for the fireplace with your "monogram" on it ("Ours alone, with bold navy initials"); you can get a fake-gold metal case designed to hold a pack of chewing gum, engraved with your initials: "Gum's more fun when you carry it in an engraved gold-tone metal case." One catalog sells sets of front-seat car mats with your full name not only in letters three inches high but enclosed in quotation marks as well, in conformity with prole usage. Or how about a navy-blue flameproof hearthrug with your family name in Gothic letters beneath seven spaced gold stars and above a golden eagle, in "Federal" style? That will certainly straighten out visitors puzzled about whose living room they've wandered into.

I don't want to make too much of the pathos of these constant assertions of selfhood, but surely there's something touching about the need to have one's "own" business card reproduced in brass, bronze, or glass on the front of one's living-room clock, or the need to have a fancy desk nameplate. Desk nameplates are *ipso facto* pathetic, favored as they are by people not certain they deserve desks, like auto salesmen, military officers, and others similarly doubtful of their status. Consider the need to use a "Personalized Book Embosser," which "seals your name and initials in every book you own. No question about whose book it is. It states 'From the Library of...'" Having a "library" itself, of course, fills a deep need, like having a "wine cellar" or fixtures implying one. Thus the carafe obtainable by mail reading "Vin Maison_____," with the blank filled with YOUR FAMILY NAME, or the wine set "for two," which adds to the personalized carafe two glasses with the couple's first names on them. If now and then something should whisper that it's not really classy to advertise your name all the time, you can still do it slightly undercover, the way the upper-middle class get its initials onto the station-wagon door by expressing them in yacht signal flags: you can order a silver "cartouche" in the Tutankhamen tradition with your name spelled out but in "hiero-glyphics." This item is to be worn on a chain around the neck: "Let It Adorn You as It Might an Egyptian Sovereign." The housewife who puts up the soothing plaque in her kitchen can also invest in a stoneware pie dish reading "Pies by Karen" (any name available). One wants to weep. And by the way, if you want to get an idea of which names for children the middle class imagines have status, you can learn a lot from the names stamped on the children's pencils illus-trated. They are heavy with British "romance" over-tones: for girls, Stacy and Kimberley; for boys, Brian, Jason, and Matthew. There are a very few occasions when *The Official Preppy Handbook* goes off the rails, but one is surely when it recommends initials and monograms as in any way classy (satire may be in-tended, but I don't think so). No matter what class exhibits them, monograms suggest some doubt about one's importance, some need to impress an audience. Actually, if you're securely upper-middle-class, your name should appear nowhere but on checks and typed underneath (illegible) signatures.

If personalizing isn't absolutely indispensable to Americans, buying things from catalogs seems to be, not because they want the things but because they need to exercise the illusion of choice by buying them. Catalog buying delivers the illusion of power without the social risk of encounters with others who might dispute your power. The act of ordering unnecessary objects by mail is a new secret way of performing what Veblen calls "the conspicuously wasteful honorific expenditure that confers spiritual well-being." In certain moods, when we wonder what we're about and what we're worth, we all resemble Billy Pilgrim's mother. "Like so many Americans," says Kurt Vonnegut, "she was trying to construct a life that made sense from things she found in gift shops."

THE LIFE OF THE MIND

IN THE ABSENCE OF A SYSTEM OF HEREDITARY RANKS and titles, without a tradition of honors conferred by a monarch, and with no well-known status ladder even of high-class regiments to confer various degrees of cachet, Americans have had to depend for their mechanism of snobbery far more than other peoples on their college and university hierarchy. In this country, just about all that's finally available as a fount of honor is the institution of the higher learning. Or at least its topmost reaches. I once heard a man with a B.A., an M.A., and a Ph.D. designated as inestimably fine with the words "He's Yale all the way." Granted, it's not much on which to base a scheme of invidious distinction, but in the long run it's virtually all we have.

As we saw when considering rear-window stickers in cars, the credit of even fairly undistinguished colleges is remarkably high, and something even of the sacred seems to attend their identities. Indeed, as institutions everyone honors they seem to outrank the church—no one puts a sticker in the car window reading "Sodality of the Holy Name, Port Huron, Michigan," or "First Baptist Church of Elmira." You can estimate the current prestige of the higher-educational establishment by considering the way everyone wants to imitate it. When an institution devoted to profit or deception or huckstering wants to elevate its status, it pretends to be a university. Thus the *New York Times* with not just its daily pedagogic solemnity but its "Weekly News Quiz," as if it were in the education business. (What other newspaper would solemnly print the following, which appeared in the *Times* for November 2, 1982: "An article ... Saturday incorrectly stated the number of positions possible for the Rubik's Cube. It is 43,252,003,274,489,856,000.") Similarly, the brokerage and real-estate rackets conduct "seminars." The most naked lobbies in Washington, those most deeply dyed in the practices of bribery and coercion, like to call themselves institutes, as if they were the Institute for Advanced Study at Princeton or the Institute of Contemporary Art at the University of Pennsylvania. Thus in the Nation's Capital we find the Tobacco Institute, the Alcoholic Beverage Institute, the Institute of Shortening and Edible Oils, and the like. Some "institutes" even have "chairs" and "professorships." As a contributor's note in a magazine tells us, one scribbler "holds the DeWitt Wallace Chair in Communications at the American Enterprise Institute."

The lust of all classes to acquire status by attaching themselves to universities, learned societies, "science," and the like—anything but commerce and manufacturing and "marketing"—can be seen in the way, for example, the Morgan Library attracts contributors of money by designating them not Donors or Benefactors, but "Fellows." And in various grades depending on amounts: the highest in rank are "Fellow in Perpetuity" (suggesting either "tenure" or the concept Perpetual Care at your local cemetery). Below these are "Honorary Fellows," then "Life Fellows," and finally just plain "Fellows."

So high is the prestige of American colleges and universities that they have been remarkably immune to criticism and contumely, at least since the 1940s when, because of the GI Bill, they were sold to the popular mind as the most high-minded part of the general postwar social-welfare system. For years few but Senator McCarthy in the 1950s and radical students in the 1960s and 1970s have pointed very vigorously to their defects and pretensions. The result is that the most preposterous affectations of these institutions have gone unrebuked, so unwilling has criticism been to risk accusations of anti-intellectualism. (As if *intellect* were a relevant commodity in any but a tiny group of these institutions.) Attempts to discriminate vigorously among the colleges are met with a special kind of horror and outrage. Pointing to the class system in institutions is for many as offensive as pointing to it in "real life."

Instructive is one response to Edward B. Fiske's *The New York Times Selective Guide to American Colleges, 1982-83* (1982). Noting that the United States has almost two thousand institutions calling themselves four-year colleges and awarding bachelor's degrees, Fiske assumed, as any intelligent person would, that few of that swollen and pretentious number could be much good. In a world where *institute* has lost its meaning, it's logical to suspect that *college* has lost its meaning too. Fiske thus set to work to identify the "best and most interesting" of American colleges, and came up with only 265. To rank academic quality, social activity, and "quality of life" at these institutions, he employed a system of five down to one stars for each criterion. The five stars he awarded Amherst, Williams, Harvard, Stanford, Smith, and others for academic quality might be seen as the equivalent of the three stars awarded by the *Guide Michelin* for excellence in the cuisine, and which signify: *"Une des meilleures tables de France: vaut le voyage."* The four stars he gave Beloit College, Bowdoin, the University of Iowa, Vanderbilt, and others are equal roughly to the Michelin's two-star ranking: *"Table excellente, mérite un détour."* The three stars he awarded Mills College, Colby, the Universities of New Hampshire and Connecticut, and others in that class would equate with Michelin's one star: *"Une bonne table dans sa catégorie."* As he canvassed the whole college scene comparatively—and fearlessly—Fiske couldn't help noticing certain institutions which in academic quality seemed to earn fewer than three stars. Like an honest critic of anything else, books, say, or plays, or even restaurants, he designated these. Some of the two-stars are Xavier University in New Orleans, Tuskegee, Temple, Seton Hall, St. Louis University, the University of Rhode Island, and Ohio Wesleyan. And to some colleges Fiske found he could award only one star for academic quality, like the University of Tulsa, the University of Oklahoma, and the University of Nebraska. Even these, however, were to a degree singled out for praise, as you realize when you discover that Fiske was unable to find a single institution of mentionable intellectual quality in the whole states of Nevada, North and South Dakota (which together have twenty "colleges"), Wyoming, and West Virginia (with seventeen candidates). Neither Richard Nixon's alma mater (Whittier College, California) nor Ronald Reagan's (Eureka College, Illinois) gets so much as a look-in.

Given the fury occasioned by any honest evaluation of universities, we might expect the governors of the states of Nevada, the Dakotas, Wyoming, and West Virginia to round on Fiske with all the *ad hominem* innuendoes at their command, accusing him of bias, blindness, snobbery, Eastern establishmentarianism (Fiske is education editor of the *New York Times*), contempt for the West, and related defects of character unfitting him for the critical office. Advertising and promotion of their fiefs have long been important obligations of governors, and we wouldn't be surprised to see them defend to the death the educational prestige of their states. But we wouldn't expect outrage from a mere professor at one of the lower-ranked institutions, for professors are supposed to understand the nature of criticism—to know that it consists of opinion, and that the more opinions, and the livelier, the better. To get into a lather about your own university's being down-graded by some newspaper employee suggests that you are in the public-relations rather than the intellect business and that, even worse, you have no great confidence in the status of your institution.

I'm speaking about David H. Bennett, Professor of History at Syracuse University. Doubtless expecting an institution where he taught to be ranked five or four stars for academic quality, he was appalled to find Fiske giving Syracuse only *two*. This ranking was in part the result of some questionnaires filled in by students as well as private interviews with them. The information they provided led Fiske to write that "the College of Arts and Sciences...is undistinguished," "classes are large," "registration is a mess," "the library...is understocked," "admissions standards tend not to be very rigorous," and "varsity sports are big," and to observe that too much teaching is done by graduate assistants. The students consulted were so demoralized as to tell Fiske, "Anyone who can pay the price gets in." Receiving this ill report from the customers, Fiske understandably brought in a mere two-star finding. Professor Bennett's reaction was not to set about redressing these defects—cleaning up the registration mess, for example, or reforming the teaching-assistant scandal, a widespread disgrace in this country. His reaction was to condemn the person and the process that had exposed these weaknesses, to find fault with the messenger who had merely borne the bad news. He wrote a letter to the messenger's boss, Arthur Ochs Sulzberger, publisher of the *New York Times*, complaining that "the social and cultural authority of the world's most respected newspaper" had been misused to lend weight to Fiske's "dubious enterprise." As he wrote Sulzberger, "*The New York Times Selective Guide* would be dismissed as a bad joke...if only it did not bear the name of your newspaper."

Addressing himself to this important question of the prestige of Syracuse University and the degree to which it had sustained damage as a result of Edward Fiske's observations, Arthur Ochs Sulzberger hastened to assure Professor Bennett that changes in the Fiske book were being made, changes which would be reflected immediately in new printings. In his reply, Sulzberger went on, however, to praise Fiske and his assistants, and to call attention to the probity and intelligence of numerous professional consultants. Nevertheless, he then indicated, despite all this he had come to the conclusion that "future printings and editions" of Fiske's book would not carry the name of the *Times* in the title. In announcing that he would withdraw the name of the newspaper from the title in future, Sulzberger was doubtless acting on the assumption that for one institution of the higher learning to criticize another is professionally unseemly.

The whole affair will give you some idea of the prestige invested in academic institutions, their tenderness to slight or disregard, their jealous pursuit of honor. Their sensitivity to slight suggests that they are what we have now instead of knights, or even gentlemen. Fiske's real offense was the word *selective*, which blew the whistle on the polite fiction that if a thing calls itself a *college* or a *university*, it is one. The scandal he occasioned was to imply how very little meaning attaches to the statement "He (or she) is a college graduate," words that, long years ago, might have carried some weight. But by the 1950s the scene had changed. The rush to attend college for status purposes soon resulted in the fate that overtook the concept *the dollar*. The word remained unchanged while the reality altered drastically.

The assumption that "a college degree" means something without the college's being specified is woven so deeply into the American myth that it dies very hard, even when confronted with the facts of the class system and its complicity with the hierarchies of the higher learning. For example: Vance Packard, in *The Status Seekers*, was persuaded as late as 1959 that the idea of "a college diploma" carried sufficient meaning to justify the class designation "the Diploma Elite." Quite wrong. To represent affairs accurately, you'd have to designate an "*Elite* Diploma Elite," because having a degree from Amherst or Williams or Harvard or Yale should never be confused with having one from Eastern Kentucky University or Hawaii Pacific College or Arkansas State or Bob Jones. Packard obfuscates the facts when he says, "A college girl is six times as likely to marry a college man as a non-college girl," which fatally ignores the flagrant unlikelihood of a man from Dartmouth marrying a girl from Nova College, Fort Lauderdale. As late as 1972 Packard is still taking that rosy egalitarian view and thus still making the same essential mistake. In *A Nation of Strangers* he writes cheerfully, "In 1940 about 13 percent of college-age young people actually went to college; by 1970 it was about 43 percent." But no. It was still about 13 percent, the other 30 percent attending things merely denominated colleges. These poor kids and their parents were performing the perpetual American quest not for intellect but for respectability and status. That the number of young people really going to college will always be about 13 percent would seem to be the message of Edward Fiske's "selective" findings.

Vance Packard is not the only one to be duped by the fraudulent semantics so common when we enter the atmosphere of the higher learning. In his book *Showing Off in America* John Brooks also opts for the pleasing appearance: he distinguishes "the two basic American classes, the college-educated and the not-college-educated." But the only meaningful educational distinction today is that between the college-educated and the "college"-educated. Richard Boyer and David Savageau's intelligent *Places Rated Almanac* (1981) gets it right. In evaluating a secondary school, "It is no longer noteworthy," they say, "that a majority of a high school's graduating class goes on to college. The question to ask is: Which colleges are accepting them—top-rated universities and colleges, or institutions with low entrance requirements?"

One of the saddest social groups today consists of that 30 percent that during the 1950s and 1960s struggled to "go to college" and thought they'd done that, only to find their prolehood still unredeemed, and not merely intellectually, artistically, and socially, but economically as well. In *Social Standing in America*, Coleman and Rainwater found that going to a good college—or in my view, a real one—increased one's income by 52 percent, while going to a really good one, like one of Fiske's five-stars, increased it by an additional 32 percent over that. But they found that you achieved "no income advantage" if you graduated from a "nonselective" college, that is, one of the roughly 1,728 institutions left decently unmentioned by Fiske. No income advantage at all.

Sometimes the middle class and the proles catch on to the college swindle (forgive the expression), but too late. I know a woman who graduated with a well-above-average record from an intellectually undemanding university only to be brutally taxed with "ignorance" by her colleagues when she began working in a vigorously competitive context in New York. She had the temerity—and bully for her, I say—to write the university president complaining bitterly, and quite effectively, about the way she'd been had. But usually awareness of the great college-and-status hoodwink goes unexpressed. It festers inside, producing a gnawing feeling that something's wrong somewhere and that one is, as usual, being screwed. Entering some backwater college convinced, as one person told Coleman and Rainwater, that "you have to go to college to be respected," the candidate emerges four years later to find he's not respected at all because his college has no clout. Despite appearances of open access, the truth is as Paul Blumberg perceives: "The educational system has been effectively appropriated by the upper strata and transformed into an instrument which tends to reproduce the class structure and transmit inequality." One reason is that a higher proportion than ever of top-class youths go to college, and they tend to go to the good places. They go to Swarthmore, while the proles go to Carlow College, Pittsburgh. The result is no surprise to members of the upper-middle class, although it may astonish the middles and the proles. "The newly arrived, eager, upwardly mobile person," says Leonard Reissman, "sweaty from his climb up the class ladder, wipes his brow and learns that the doors to full recognition and acceptance are still closed to him." Of course, a cynic might comment, because the effect of the whole system is to stabilize class rigidity under the color of opening up genuine higher learning to everyone.

How was so bold a class deception accomplished? Was it intentional or accidental? It happened largely during the Kennedy and Johnson administrations, under the laudable, if unwittingly ironic, guise of "opening up educational opportunity." If that commodity were in rich supply and available for simple purchase, the scheme might have succeeded. But intelligence and learning and curiosity are, regrettably, rarer than some imagine, and you don't bring people into contact with them simply by announcing that you're doing it. "Educational opportunity" was opened up by the process of verbal inflation, by promoting, that is, numerous normal schools, teachers colleges, provincial "theological seminaries," trade schools, business schools, and secretarial institutes to the name and status of "universities," thus conferring on them an identity they were by no means equipped to bear, or even understand. The process was analogous to the way high-school students are finally extruded to enter "college," and for both processes one description can serve: unearned promotion. What was happening in the 1960s was simply an acceleration of a process normal in this country—inflation, hyperbole, bragging. As one citizen exulted in the 1970s: "There are two universities in England, four in France, ten in Prussia, and thirty-seven in Ohio." Here it's as natural for every college to want to be a university as for every employee to want to be an "executive," and every executive a vice president.

The result? State colleges and teachers colleges all over the country were suddenly denominated universities, and they set to work, with the best motives in the world, ripping off the proles. Southern Illinois University is a good example of the genre. Formerly a mere teachers college, it now enrolls 26,000 students and has its own "university press," although it's located in Carbondale, Illinois, a backwater without significant intellectual meaning or cultural tradition. The giveaway is that the largest number of bachelor's degrees issued by Southern Illinois University is still in "education," an immediate sign not of a university but of what used to be called, more honestly, a normal school. The same observations would hold true of hundreds of places like Ball State, Kent State, Wright State University (Dayton, Ohio), and the University of Northern Iowa.

Many TV viewers of a recent national basketball championship must have been as puzzled as I was to identify "James Madison University," which was playing the University of North Carolina. This institution, located in Harrisonburg, Virginia, until recently was Madison College, a modest teacher-training outfit. It has been promoted now to a status bringing it into comparison with Oxford and the Sorbonne, but it still specializes in elementary education, and the average verbal score on the Scholastic Aptitude Test of its freshmen is a subacademic 455 for the men, 463 for the women. One frivolous but not entirely untrustworthy guide to college quality might be the absence of a given college from national basketball tournaments. At least this might seem to follow from the constant appearance there of such as the University of Dayton, DePaul, Virginia Tech, the University of Wyoming (remember Fiske's findings about Wyoming?), Seton Hall University, and Bradley University. Sports commentators who refer to these places as "schools" ("——— is a great basketball school") usually denominate them more accurately than the state governments that award them charters as universities. And in the private sector we have Fairleigh Dickinson University in New Jersey, a junior college until the 1940s, when the GI Bill and veterans' money encouraged it to redesignate itself. Only nine years were needed for a Seattle business school to achieve university status. Founded in 1973, "City College," this institution proclaims in 1982, "has grown to be a university," suggesting that size is the determinant. The sad thing is that there are innocent people around who will believe it's what it calls itself.

The process of reasoning by which these institutions are conceived and born sometimes resembles the following. If universities are named for *places* elsewhere, like Oxford and Cambridge, if there are such things as the University of Paris and the University of London, why not put our places on the map and even confer a similar dignity on them by inventing things called the University of Evansville, or the University of Dallas, or of Houston, or of Louisville? What does it matter that no spirit of learning is visible in the place? What does it matter if curiosity and study are unknown there, or if the very idea of intellectual rigor and excellence makes people nervous and insecure?

This promotion of colleges to universities is consistent with the long-honored American custom (more on this later) of "raising" a thing by adding to the number of syllables used to describe it. For example, *rain* is raised to *precipitation*. *College* has only two syllables, and even *seminary* only four. But *university*, with five syllables, adds distinction. Thus:

> University of Montevallo, Alabama
> Samford University, Alabama
> West Coast University, California
> Woodbury University, California
> Upper Iowa University

Transylvania University, Kentucky
Shaw University, North Carolina
Cameron University, Oklahoma
Phillips University, Oklahoma
Midwestern University, Texas
Pan American University, Texas

And this merely scratches the surface. Why are so many of these located in places kindness itself would have to recognize as less-favored parts of the country? The answer is that many began as little church colleges named after Bible Belt preachers which finally added to themselves tiny illiterate, harebrained theological schools, thus sanctioning the "university" title. And considerably below these, there's the real bottom, where universities no one's heard of shade off into the ones that are outright frauds, the ones that award fake "doctorates" in exchange for cash and a written deposition about one's "life experiences." Since in this

A SCENE COMMON SINCE THE 1950s

country there's hardly an easier exercise than denominating anything a university, the buyer must constantly beware. In Washington, D.C., itself, there's the Maharishi International University College of Natural Law. And the rich are just as gullible as the poor. Witness one intellectually unheard-of university in the Northeast whose annual tuition ($7,100 in 1980) puts it among the ten most costly in the United States, right up there with Yale, M.I.T., Stanford, Princeton, and Harvard.

It's not hard to understand the way these feeble institutions take root and grow into plausibility. Near where I live there's a large acreage which has somehow escaped having "garden apartments" built all over it. Except for a few buildings in the middle, the land is, as yet, empty. Years ago, a sign by the roadside identified the buildings as belonging to the "Consolata Fathers." A few years later a great brick building with an arched roof began to go up, together with an adjacent structure resembling a "dormitory." The sign now reads "Consolata Missionaries," and one fears that something big is about to take place. I'll predict what's going to happen, and very soon, too. A few more buildings will be erected, and then an imposing entryway gate with a sign, "Consolata College," will appear. A few years later, more buildings, and overnight the sign will change to "Consolata University," the institution now proving its right to that title by a notable basketball team, marching band, and drill team, as well as wheelchair ramps everywhere and special programs for the handicapped. There will be a plethora of programs abroad: Consolata in Palermo, Consolata in Kusadisi, Consolata in Hyderabad. Then, before you know it, you'll be seeing, in *The New York Review of Books*, ads for books published by the Consolata University Press, books with titles like *Structuralism and George*

Eliot's Dilemma and *The Missing Marxist Dimension in the Writings of Samuel Johnson.* Consolata University will then seem as serious as any other, and no one will think its sudden efflorescence at all funny.

The proliferation of questionable colleges at the bottom makes the selective few at the top even more valuable as status devices, for there are proportionately fewer of them and their programs are safely liberal, their standards secure. Because of their stuffy and uncompromising distinction, invidious comparisons can still be conveniently drawn, as in the remark you can hear around New England and the Mid-Atlantic states: "He's college but not Ivy." But the very topmost classes, having no need for this kind of cachet, are largely *hors de université.* We can say of their expectations of their children what Douglas Sutherland says of the English gentleman's: his offspring "are expected to conform in all things, and academic brilliance is not an acceptable deviation from the normal." This attitude is entirely consistent with the pose of the amateur enjoined on those classes that don't have to earn money. It's a disgrace to be in any way professional, and thus, says Sutherland, "a gentleman never looks under the bonnet of his motor car, for he makes a point of knowing nothing about engines." For numerous reasons, then, top-out-of-sights and uppers most often send their kids to dubious institutions— partly out of sheer ignorance; partly defensively, knowing their children can't get into good ones; and partly out of sheer eccentricity and stubbornness. Cornelius Vanderbilt Whitney again provides the example. His daughter and her friends go not to Vassar or Wellesley or even Northeastern or Wheaton but to Boca Raton College, Florida. He has no sense that there's anything anomalous about this, noting at one point how much he and his wife have enjoyed touring the nearby "Embry-Riddle Aeronautical University, where I got my Doctoral degree last December." At lunch there, he reports, "We were introduced to everyone as Doctor Whitney and Doctor Whitney, my wife, Mary, having received a degree of Doctor of Humane Letters at the American University in Leysin, Switzerland."

On the other hand, archaic and good colleges like Princeton and Yale are used for status definition and support by exemplary Americans of the upper-middle and middle class like F. Scott Fitzgerald and John O'Hara. Although neither managed to graduate from the top-class college of his choice, and although O'Hara never even got to attend his, pursuing for life the fantasy that he might have gone to Yale and leafing through the yearbook for 1924, which would have been his class, both promoted their colleges to the status of holy places, sacred sodalities to which they could redeem themselves by belonging. Each would have affixed his rear-window sticker with utmost reverence. They were team players both, like so many members of the middle class, and could hardly imagine their identity unless attached to an institution.

The social implications of the better colleges are nicely registered in Philip Roth's *Goodbye, Columbus* (1959), where, in contrast to the streets of prole Newark, those of upper-middle Short Hills are recalled by the narrator as named after classy colleges, like Amherst, Bowdoin, Cornell, Dartmouth, Harvard, etc. *The Social Register* finds that it must mention the same colleges so often that it uses a table of abbreviations to ease its work. The Ivies of course are all there, but so are Hobart, Lehigh, C.C.N.Y., Rensselaer Polytechnic, and Rutgers. To be sure, some of the prestige of the Ivy has diminished in the popular if not the upper-middle-class mind. If two ships plied today between Los Angeles and San Francisco, it's doubtful that the company running them would seek to give them class, as it did a half century ago, by naming them the *Harvard* and the *Yale*. But Ivy still extends an irresistible appeal to the upper-middle class, and even if you don't get in there, it's essential to "go away"—preferably some distance—to college (unless you happen to live in Cambridge, New Haven, Princeton, Providence, Hanover, or the like). But those who postpone Ivy ambitions until college-admission time are already in class arrears, as C. Wright Mills perceives: "Harvard or Yale or Princeton is not enough. It is the really exclusive prep school that counts...," and unless one's gone to Hotchkiss, Groton, Hill, St. Mark's, Andover, Exeter, or Milton, the whole Ivy college act's likely to be socially a waste. The wits of *The Preppy Handbook* know how important it is to go to a good prep school, especially one known to be an efficient "feed" into the Ivy. The right school's crucial because "you want to...go to the best [college] possible so that you can forever after wave your handkerchief or beat your breast during the last stanza of certain songs." "It is not enough to succeed," says Gore Vidal; "others must fail." It is not enough that there be a Williams College; there must also be a University of Southern Mississippi to give it value, so that both may play their parts in the great American class system of the higher learning.

It is funny, to be sure, that Americans must depend upon the system of higher education for purposes of invidious class competitiveness. It is funny that to protect that purpose, the prestige of the upper parts of the system must be defended by such as Professor Bennett from exposure and devaluation. If these things are comic, there are other things about the system that are not at all funny. The psychological damage wrought by this incessant struggle for status is enormous just because of the extraordinary power of these institutions to confer prestige. The number of hopes blasted and hearts broken for class reasons is probably greater in the world of colleges and universities than anywhere else. And that's true not just of students and aspirant students, kids who aim at Columbia but get admitted to Ohio Wesleyan instead. It's true of professors as well. I've never actually known a college teacher who killed himself or others because he lost status by not being retained at a "most selective" institution and had to move to a "highly selective" or merely "very selective" one. But I've known many college teachers thus ruined by shame and convictions of inadequacy, who thenceforth devoted their lives to social envy and bitterness rather than wit and scholarship. Anyone who doesn't realize that, whether for their attenders or their conductors, colleges and universities are the current equivalent of salons and levees and courts should look harder. If no other institution here confers the titles of nobility forbidden by the Constitution, they do. Or something very like it.

Whether you learn to read at a good or bad college or at a good or bad prep school or high school, what you read is an almost infallible class signal. (And whether you read at all. "The divisions between those who read and write and those who don't," says Tom Wolfe, "are taking on a great social significance.") The taste in reading of the upper classes is soon dispatched. C. Wright Mills is correct when he observes that although they may display books, they tend not to read them except books on "management" and copious mystery and detective narratives, forgotten as soon as consumed. They read magazines mostly, precisely those John T. Molloy recommends disposing about the office waiting room to convey an upper-middle-class air: *Time*, *Newsweek*, and *U.S. News & World Report*; and *For-*

tune, Forbes, Business Week, Barron's, and *Dun's Review*. If you're an author and you give one of your books to a member of the upper class, you must never expect him to read it.

Nor will the matter of prole reading tastes delay us long. Here the favored commodities are the high-prole *Reader's Digest* (circulation 17.87 million) and *TV Guide* (17.67 million), together with dailies like the *New York Daily News* and mid- and low-prole weeklies like the *National Enquirer, Weekly World News, Star,* and *Globe,* which you pick up at the supermarket. At first glance, the popularity of all these last will seem to argue a total breakdown in public secondary education, so full are they of medieval wonders, magic, and sheer quasi-scientific nonsense—creatures from outer space, out-of-body "travel," and the triumphs of psychics. But a closer look suggests that the editor's tongue is very often in the cheek, producing a highly sophisticated form of play back and forth across the border normally thought to distinguish fantasy from actuality. "Hitler, aged 93, behind Argentinian invasion of Falklands," one reads, or "Top Scientists Talk with the Dead." Each week's harmless wonder effaces the one before, and these sensations do as little real damage as the "predictions" and the advice about marriage and the family. The prole weeklies also offer their readers the comfort of lots of gossip about the secret lives of the celebrated. The point, like barroom pedantry about sports, is to provide the prole with an illusion of power, giving him a sense that it is he who controls the famous, or at least that it is he who determines which ones will succeed and fail. But full as they may be of wonders and scandal, the essential function of the prole weeklies is to soothe and comfort. No one whatever, we realize, is trying to stir up the proles to rebellion:

COFFEE AND ALCOHOL CAN HELP YOU LOSE
WEIGHT

HOORAY FOR THE U.S.A. (Life in the U.S. has
been getting better and better—and it will keep on
improving in the future!)

The method, dear to the prole sensibility, is to take an
opinion and proclaim it a fact. Sometimes the object
is to cheer the aged, the timid, and the discouraged by
examples of bravery and virtue or by presumed good
news about "immortality":

TO PROVE I WASN'T OVER THE HILL AT 72, I
SAILED ACROSS THE ATLANTIC—ALONE.

SHARECROPPER AND WIFE PUT THEIR 12
CHILDREN THROUGH COLLEGE.

MOST U.S. CONGRESSMEN BELIEVE IN LIFE
AFTER DEATH.

Lest, contemplating these, we're tempted to assume
unwarranted airs of superiority, it's well to remember
that the prole weeklies have no lien on lunacy. Here's
an ad appearing in *The New Republic*, presumably addressed, like the rest of that estimable journal, to ra-
tionalists, liberals, "college graduates," and wits:

JESUS FICTIONAL! Positive proof Flavius
Josephus created Jesus, authored Gospels.
Booklet, $3.00...

and in the same issue,

The End is Near! Find out. Send $1.00...

As readers, proles are honest, never trying to fake effects or simulate interest in higher things. It's among the middle class that tastes in reading get really interesting, because it's only here that pretense, fraud, and misrepresentation enter. The uppers don't care what you think about their reading, and neither do the proles. The poor anxious middle class is the one that wants you to believe it reads "the best literature," and condemnatory expressions like *trash* or *rubbish* are often on its lips. It is the natural audience for the unreadable second-rate pretentious, books by James Gould Cozzens, John Steinbeck, Pearl Buck, Lawrence Durrell's *Alexandria Quartet*, the mass merchandise of Herman Wouk, John Hersey, and Irwin Shaw, and the Durants' history of philosophy. A middle classic to perfection is *The Old Man and the Sea*, which Hemingway virtually was obliged to write, Thornton Wilder having stopped producing and thus leaving a gap to be filled. The middle class is mad for Dylan Thomas—Jimmy Carter deposed that he was his favorite poet—in large part because the records of his readings de-ideologize poems, transforming them into something like stereo music. It is in the middle-class dwelling that you're likely to spot the fifty-four-volume set of the Great Books, together with the half-witted two-volume Syntopicon, because the middles, the great audience for how-to books, believe in authorities. Thus it serves as the classic market for encyclopedias. Displayed in the maple wall hutch along with the collectibles will be the most recent transmissions from the Book-of-the-Month Club (the Literary Guild, if you went to a worse college; volumes of *Reader's Digest Condensed Books* if you didn't go at all).

Naturally the middle class is addicted to nonideological periodicals, nice ones like the *National Geographic*, *Smithsonian*, and *House & Garden*. National

UPPER-MIDDLE

MIDDLE

PROLE

WHAT SOME OF THE CLASSES LIKE TO TAKE IN

Geographic also offers the middle class the upper-middle-class fantasy of sending a refractory, dope-sodden son away to one of the expensive military schools or disciplinary camps advertised in the back pages. *Psychology Today* gives the middle class the illusion that it has up-to-date scientific interests, and *The New Yorker* persuades it that it cares about culture and the finer things, like Steuben glass. Where proles would read *Popular Mechanics*, the middle class, having graduated from college, goes in for *Science Digest*. The more liberal a member of the middle class imagines himself, the more likely that *Consumer Reports* will be displayed somewhere. The designers of the mail-order catalogs have learned that all their customers like to be thought devotees of reading matter about their station. One middle-class catalog aimed at daily readers of, say, the *New Brunswick* (New Jersey) *Home News* advertises a fancy doormat. On the mat, folded, appears the *New York Times*. The same catalog exhorts the reader to "Keep newspapers neat and ready to bind for recycling" and illustrates with a photograph of a wrought-iron rack with newspapers stacked up in it. Is the topmost, visible paper the *Omaha World-Herald*? No, it's the *Wall Street Journal*. Following the same practice, a high-prole catalog peddling fake-"Western" reproduction antique furniture shows a chairside magazine rack containing *Atlantic Monthly*, *The New Yorker*, and *Smithsonian*, rather than the *Family Circle* and *Field & Stream* we'd expect to find there.

We must not leave the topic of the reading of the middle class without noting the impact of its audienceship on American prose style. Its terror of ideology, opinion, and sharp meaning, which we've seen before in its visual tastes, are the main cause of the euphemism, jargon, gentility, and verbal slop that wash over us. The middle-class anxiety about the "controversial" is the reason *The New Yorker* rarely runs unfavorable book reviews: too upsetting to the clientele, the way piquant, pointed prose might be. Better for language first to ingratiate and finally, by waffling, vagueness, and evasion, to stay out of trouble altogether. The prose demanded by the middle class is preeminently that of institutional advertising, and it's manufactured by the most cunning corporations to imitate the *faux-naif* sound of *The New Yorker*'s "Talk of the Town." The Mobil Oil Corporation is skilled in act, going in for just-folks confessions of ignorance ("we didn't know . . . either") and assertions of the banal, as if avoidance of it invited accusations of elitism. "The world did not come to an end on Wednesday, March 10 [1982], as some people had feared," it tells us in an ad a week later:

> True, the planets were aligned in syzygy on that day—meaning that they were all on the same side of the sun. (We didn't know the meaning of the word syzygy either, so we looked it up. . . .) If the world isn't coming to an end in the foreseeable future, why not make it a better place in which to live?

That last will remind us of the indispensability of cliché to middle-class understanding. Where the more fortunately educated read to be surprised, the middle class reads to have its notions confirmed, and deviations from customary verbal formulas disconcert and annoy it.

The middle class is predominantly the audience for the numerous "new translations" (*rewritings* would be a better term) of the Bible which stigmatize our age. It's notable that these new versions were not thought necessary until universal education was said to have become widespread. So unfortunately educated as to be puzzled by any form of English but the contemporary, with no sense of the history not just of ideas but of styles and idiom, the middle class requires that even its divinity be couched in "language that is easy to understand." If, as Auden says,

> Time...
> Worships language, and forgives
> Everyone by whom it lives,

the middle class hates and fears language, and in effect it insists that a class separation take place between those who relish

> Whither thou goest, I will go
>   (Ruth, I, 16)

and the version they like,

> Where you go, I will go.

Equipped thus by different educations and expectations and mental atmospheres, the classes will not just read different things. Largely as a result of their reading, they will believe different things, and it's this as much as anything that makes the United States, as Richard Polenberg calls it in his book, *One Nation Divisible* (1980). The two top classes, as we've seen, have very few ideas. One of the few is that capital must never be "invaded," as it likes to put it. Another is that a jacket and tie are never to be omitted. But other than those, it has no very extensive stock of beliefs. It doesn't even believe in culture, like the upper-middle class; or if it does, it likes culture accompanied by other goodies too. Cornelius Vanderbilt Whitney likes Saratoga Springs because, he finds, "there are the Arts and the best horse racing in the U.S.A." Aspen, Colorado, is a cultural mecca for the upper class not just because it's costly to get to but because there you can have culture, and "scenery" and leisure-class sports at the same time.

The middle class, on the other hand, has lots of beliefs. It still believes in constipation, for example, holding that if you don't "have a bowel movement" daily, you're in deep trouble and should immediately swallow a "laxative," preferably one advertised on TV. Just as it hopes to fend off criticism by keeping its kitchens spotlessly clean, so does the middle class with its bowels, lest some shameful dirtiness be inferred. "I'm studying colon therapy," one young woman told Studs Terkel: "our system isn't clean." Other middle-class beliefs are that one ought to be a professional at all costs, because being a dentist or a vet is nobler than being a salaried employee; that nothing wears like leather; that you are judged by your luggage; and that you should dress up for traveling. It believes that Peter Shaffer is a profound playwright, probably the equal of Shakespeare (the way Durrell is the equal of "Prowst"), and it's likely to stand and applaud at the end of the psychiatrist's speech in *Equus*. It holds architectural views, and thinks the opera house at Lincoln Center beautiful, what with all the gold and crimson and little lights. (Brief examination in passing: are you sent to an extraordinary degree by the cuckoo in Beethoven's *Pastoral Symphony*? Then you're middle-class.) It believes that an "air terminal" is higher in class than a bus station, and its commitment to the imagery of efficiency and progress leads it to believe that a household or personal computer will solve its problems. (That's a middle-class version of the prole belief in "debt consolidation.") This middle-class belief in electronic solutions of human problems is celebrated in a very plausible TV ad depicting a father announcing at his daughter's wedding that he's giving her a Betamax as a present. This strikes the audience—clearly middle-class—as immensely sensible.

Proles being more interesting than the middle class in almost every way, we'd expect their beliefs to be too. What middle-class person would hold the colorful belief that objects dreamed about have meanings ascertainable in a Dream Sign Book? Or that a copper bracelet will repel arthritis? Or that one has quite a good chance to win lots of money betting on horse races? Or that the authorities introduce bromide into servicemen's food to repress lust? Or that Laetrile will arrest cancer? Or that the concept *Creation Science* involves no oxymoron? Or that it's open to anyone to make a killing by "inventing" something, "an anti-gravity belt or something like that," as a Manhattan bellhop was once heard to say? Or that cripples and the deformed are really "reincarns," being punished this time around for misdemeanors committed in a previous life? Or that Esperanto is the solution to the world's misunderstandings? Or that there's nothing funny about the designation "Ladies' Auxiliary," when associated with the Elks, or the American Legion, or the Ancient Order of Hibernians? Or nothing comic, or even odd, about a tennis tournament called the Congoleum Classic? Where the middle-class heart leaps up when solicited by an ad for hideous jewelry from Tiffany, the prole responds with equal joy and hope to ads promising to alleviate rectal itch or promoting a book on poker which will earn the purchaser "a Guaranteed Income for Life."

But it's primarily in its bent toward superstition that the prole mind differs from the middle-class version. It's largely in deference to prole sensibilities that buildings have no thirteenth floor and that thirteen is skipped over when racing cars are numbered. Indeed, numbers are much in the minds of proles, just as larger numbers (with dollar signs attached) are much in the minds of the upper- and upper-middle classes: sports scores with significant meanings, lucky numbers, lottery numbers. At an airport recently I was in line at a newsstand behind a prole whose wife was standing some distance away. His purchases of a magazine and "gum" amounting to $2.65, he shouted to her, rather hoping all would hear and thus identify him as a dashing sport, "Remember sixty-five for the [lottery] number!" Proles read horoscopes avidly and take regular astrological advice. They believe that winning and losing "streaks" are actual and self-propelling, and they believe in gambling systems. Believing that supernatural intervention will help locate lost objects, they insert newspaper classifieds thanking St. Anthony for his help. They believe in heaven. They respond to direct-mail ads reading

> Do you need help??? Do you need prayer? Are you troubled? Are you lonely? Do you need a continuous flow of money blessings?...I want to mail you this "Golden Cross of Prosperity." Like I said, don't send any money.

Although it might be entertaining to follow up the implications of De Tocqueville's conclusion that "religious insanity is very common in the United States," it would be too large an undertaking for this book, nor would it be seemly here to dwell on the class significance of religious beliefs. But we can't help noticing, finally, the social meaning of the various funerary practices of the classes. Here perhaps the crucial class divide, between uppers and lowers no matter how designated, is between families who, in wintertime, provide floral "grave blankets" to keep their dead warm in their cemetery lots and those who wouldn't think of it. Another line of division separates those who go in for splendid funerals and subsequent showy newspaper In Memoriam ads, and those who don't. Jilly Cooper quotes (or devises) a classic:

> God took Dad home,
> It was His will.
> But why that way,
> We wonder still.

> Always in our thoughts. Fondest Love.
> Doris, Sharon, Auntie Edna and little Terry.

But it's kinder not to probe too deeply into such things. Better to be warned off by the high-school boy in the Middle West who told an inquiring sociologist, "Yeah, we smoke dope all over, in our cars, walking around before class, anytime, but that doesn't mean we don't believe in God or that we'll let anybody put God down."

❆[VII]❆

"SPEAK, THAT I MAY SEE THEE"

REGARDLESS OF THE MONEY YOU'VE INHERITED, THE danger of your job, the place you live, the way you look, the shape and surface of your driveway, the items on your front porch and in your living room, the sweetness of your drinks, the time you eat dinner, the stuff you buy from mail-order catalogs, the place you went to school and your reverence for it, and the materials you read, your social class is still most clearly visible when you say things. "One's speech is an unceasingly repeated public announcement about background and social standing," says John Brooks, translating into modern American Ben Jonson's observation "Language most shows a man. Speak, that I may see thee." And what held true in his seventeenth century holds even truer in our twentieth, because we now have something virtually unknown to Jonson, a sizable middle class desperate not to offend through language and thus addicted to such conspicuous class giveaways as euphemism, genteelism, and mock profanity ("Golly!").

But at the outset it's well to recognize the difficulty of talking accurately about the class significance of language. It's easy to get it wrong when talking about classes, or traditions, not one's own, the way the Englishman H. B. Brooks-Baker recently got American class usage quite wrong when he offered an "American Section" of upper- and lower-class terms in Richard Buckle's *U and Non-U Revisited* (1978). Mastery of this field takes years, and it's admittedly hard to hear accurately across the Atlantic. Still, Brooks-Baker's list of twenty-six expressions said to be avoided by upper Americans errs dramatically. For example, he tells us that *affair* is a non-upper word for *party*. But any American of any of the classes knows that the two are different things entirely, not different names for the same thing. An *affair* is a laid-on commercial catering event like a bad banquet or reception. Unlike a *party*, you don't go to an *affair* (unless it's a love affair) expecting to have a wildly good time. Again, Brooks-Baker informs the reader that *folding-stuff* is prole for *money*. No, it's simply archaic slang, as much heard today as *mazuma* or *greenbacks*. Brooks-Baker also says that in the U.S.A. proles say *tux*, uppers *tuxedo*. Wrong again. Proles say *tux*, middles *tuxedo*, but both are considered low by uppers, who say *dinner jacket* or (higher) *black tie*. But even getting our hero decently home from his *tuxedo affair* (i.e., *black-tie party*), Brooks-Baker slips up. Proles say *limo*, he asserts, uppers *limousine*. Wrong on both counts. Proles say *big black shiny Cad*, (sometimes *Caddy*). Middles say *limousine*, and the thing would be called a *limo* only behind the scenes by those who supply rented ones for funerals, bar mitzvahs, and the like. What, then, is this vehicle called by the upper orders? It's called a *car*, as in "We'll need the car about eleven, please, Parker."

Brooks-Baker's slips are useful reminders of the hazards of interpreting language class signals aright. Alexis de Tocqueville's errors in prophecy also provide a handy warning against overconfidence there. De Tocqueville overestimated the leveling force on language of "democracy," and imagined that this new kind of political organization would largely efface social distinctions in language and verbal style. Looking about him at mid-nineteenth-century America, he thought he heard everyone using the same words, and conceived that the line was ceasing to be drawn "between . . . expressions which seem by their very nature vulgar and others which appear to be refined." He concluded that "there is as much confusion in language as there is in society." But developments on this continent have proved him wrong about both language and democratic society. Actually, just *because* the country's a democracy, class distinctions have developed with greater rigor than elsewhere, and language, far from coalescing into one great central mass without social distinctions, has developed even more egregious class signals than anyone could have expected. There's really no confusion in either language or society, as ordinary people here are quite aware. Interviewed by sociologists, they indicate that speech is the main way they estimate a stranger's social class when they first encounter him. "Really," says one deponent, "the first time a person opens his mouth, you can tell."

Because the class system here is more complicated than in England, less amenable to merely binary categorization, language indicators are more numerous and subtle than merely those accepted as "U" (i.e., upper) or stigmatized as "non-U" by Nancy Mitford in her delightful 1955 essay in *Encounter*, "The English Aristocracy." Still, a way to begin considering the class meaning of language in the U.S.A. is to note some absolute class dividers. Probably the most important, a usage firmly dividing the prole classes from the middles and highers, is the double negative, as in "I can't get no satisfaction." You're as unlikely to hear something like that in a boardroom or premises frequented by "houseguests," or on a sixty-five-foot schooner off Nantucket, as you are likely to hear it in a barracks, an auto-repair shop, or a workmen's bar. Next in importance would rank special ways of managing grammatical number, as in "He don't" and "I wants it." And these are not just "slips" or "errors." They signal virtually a different dialect, identifying speakers socially distinct from users of the other English. The two can respect each other, but they can never be pals. They belong to different classes, and if they attempt to mix, they will inevitably regard each other as quaint and not quite human.

If it's grammar that draws the line between middles and below, it's largely pronunciation and vocabulary that draw it between middles and above. Everyone will have his personal collection of class indicators here, but I have found the following quite trustworthy. Words employed to register (or advertise) "cultural experience" are especially dangerous for the middle class, even *crêpes*, which they pronounce *craypes*. The same with most words deployed to display one's familiarity with the foreign, like *fiancé*, which the middle class prefers to *boyfriend* and delivers with a ridiculous heavy stress on the final syllable: *fee-on-say'*. The same with *show-fur'*, a word it prefers to the upper-class *driver*. Some may think pronouncing the *h* in *Amherst* an excessively finicking indicator of middle-classhood, but others may not. The word *diamond*, pronounced as two syllables by uppers, is likely to be rendered as three by the middle class. Similarly with *beautiful*—three syllables to uppers, but, to middles, *bee-you'-tee-full*. The "grand" words *exquisite, despicable, hospitable, lamentable* invite the middle class to stress the second syllable; those anxious to leave no doubt of their social desirability stress the first, which is also to earn some slight, passing Anglophilic credit. As the middle class gets itself more deeply entangled in artistic experience, hazards multiply, like *patina*, a word it likes a lot but doesn't realize is stressed on the first syllable. High-class names from cultural history pose a similar danger, especially if they are British, like Henry Purcell. President Reagan's former adviser Edwin Meese III clearly signaled his class when, interviewed on television, he chose to exhibit his gentility by using the word *salutary* instead of the common *wholesome* or *healthy*, but indicated by his pronunciation that he thought the word *salutory*. That's the pure middle-class act: opt for the showy, and in so doing take a pratfall. Class unfortunates who want to emphasize the largeness of something are frequently betrayed by *enormity*, as in "The whale was of such an enormity that they could hardly get it in the tank." (Prole version: "The whale was so big they couldn't hardly get it in the tank.") Elegance is the fatal temptation for the middle class, dividing it from the blunter usages of uppers and proles alike. Neither of these classes would warn against two people's simultaneously pursuing the same project by speaking of "duplicity of effort." The middle class is where you hear *prestigious* a lot, and to speculate about the reason it's replaced *distinguished* or *noted* or *respected* in the past twenty years is to do a bit of national soul-searching. The implications of *prestige*, C. Wright Mills observes, are really pejorative: "In its origins," he says, "it means dazzling the eye with conjuring tricks." And he goes on: "In France, 'prestige' carries an emotional association of fraudulence, of the art of illusion, or at least of something adventitious." The same in Italy and Germany. Only in the U.S.A. does the word carry any prestige, and looking back, I see that I've depended on *prestige* quite a lot when talking about high-class colleges.

Some of these class dividers are crude. Others are subtle. The upper and upper-middle classes have a special vocabulary for indicating wearisome or unhappy social situations. They say *tiresome* or *tedious* where their social inferiors would say *boring*; they say *upset* or *distressed* or even *cross* where others would say *angry* or *mad* or *sore*. There's a special upper-class diction of approval too. No prole man would call something *super* (Anglophilic) or *outstanding* (prep school), just as it would sound like flagrant affectation for a prole woman to designate something seen in a store as *divine* or *darling* or *adorable*. *Nice* would be the non-upper way of putting it.

But it's the middle-class quest for grandeur and gentility that produces the most interesting effects. As we've seen, imported words especially are its downfall. It will speak of a *graffiti* and it thinks *chauvinism* has something to do with gender aggression. Pseudo-classical plurals are a constant pitfall: the middles will speak learnedly of *a phenomena* and *a criteria* and *a strata* and (referring perhaps to a newspaper) *a media*. A well-known author is *a literati*. It thinks *context* a grander form of the word *content*, and thus says things like "I didn't like the context of that book: all that blood and gore." Or consider the Coast Guard officer reporting a grievous oil spill in San Francisco Bay: *cross* is too vulgar a term for the occasion, he imagines, and so he says that "several ships transited the area." When after a succession of solecisms of this kind a middle-class person will begin to suspect that he is blowing his cover, he may try to reestablish status by appliquéing a mock-classical plural ending onto a perfectly ordinary word like *process*. Then he will say *process-sees*. The whole middle-class performance nicely illustrates the conclusion of Lord Melbourne. "The higher and lower classes, there's some good in them," he observed, "but the middle classes are all affectation and conceit and pretense and concealment."

All classes except sometimes upper-middle are implicated in the scandal of saying *home* when they mean *house*. But the middle class seems to take a special pleasure in saying things like "They live in a lovely five-hundred-thousand-dollar *home*," or, after an earthquake, "The man noticed that his *home* was shaking violently." We can trace, I think, the stages by which *house* disappeared as a word favored by the middle class. First, *home* was offered by the real-estate business as a way of warming the product, that is, making the prospect imagine that in laying out money for a house he was purchasing not a passel of bricks, Formica, and wallboard but snuggly warmth, comfort, and love. The word *home* was then fervently embraced by the customers for several reasons: (1) the middle class loves to use words which have achieved cliché status in advertising; (2) the middle class, like the real-estate con men, also enjoys the comforting fantasy that you can purchase love, comfort, warmth, etc., with cold cash, or at least achieve them by some formula or other; (3) the middle class, by nature both puritanical and terrified of public opinion, welcomed *home* because, to its dirty mind, *house* carried bad associations. One spoke of a *rest home*, but of a *bawdy*, *whore-*, *fancy*, or *sporting house*. No one ever heard of a *home of ill fame*, or, for that matter, a *cat home*. So out went *house* for the same reason that *madam* has never really caught on in middle-class America. But curiously, users of *home* to describe domestic shelters make one exception. A *beach house* is so called, never a *beach home*. Because of the word's association with current

real-estate scams, a *home*, or something appropriately
so designated, does tend to suggest something pretty
specific: namely, a small pretentious, jerry-built developer's rip-off positioned in some unfortunate part
of the country without history, depth, or allusiveness.
You don't speak of a "two-hundred-year-old white
clapboard frame farmhome" in Maine, New Hampshire, or Vermont. *Homes* are what the middle class
lives in. As it grows progressively poorer, it sells its
homes and moves into *mobile homes* (formerly, trailers) or *motor homes*.

   Home is by no means the only advertising word
embraced by the middle class. "Come into the living
forum," you may hear as the corporate wife ushers you
into the living room. Or "I think I left your coat in the
reception galleria" (front hall). Or "Would you care to
go directly up to your sleeping chamber?" And because
of its need for the illusion of power and success that
attend self-conscious consumerism, the middles instinctively adopt advertisers' *-wear* compounds, speaking with no embarrassment whatever of the family's

> footwear
> nightwear (or sleepwear)
> leisurewear
> stormwear
> beachwear
> swimwear
> citywear
> countrywear
> campuswear
> formalwear
> eyewear (i.e., spectacles)
> neckwear, etc.,

and they feel good uttering the analogous *-ware* compounds:

tableware
dinnerware
stemware
barware
flatware
kitchenware
glassware

or sometimes, when they get into their grand mood, *crystal*. (Uppers, whom the middles think they're imitating, say *glasses*.) Because it's a staple of advertising, the middle class also likes the word *designer*, which it takes to mean *beautiful* or *valuable*. Thus roll paper towels with expensive patterns printed on them cease to be stupid and ugly once they're designated *designer towels*. The Dacron bath towels of the middle class, the ones with the metallic threads, are also usually called *designer towels*.

Advertising diction feeds so smoothly into the middle-class psyche because of that class's bent toward rhetorical fake elegance. Aspiring to ascend, it imagines that verbal grandeur will forward the process. Thus *enormity*, *salutory*, *duplicity*—and of course *gourmet*. "The theater still has a certain *nicety* to it," says an actor in a TV interview. He means *delicacy*, but he also means that he's middle-class and slavering to be upper. A fine example of middle-class bogus elegance is the language of a flyer circulated recently to advertise a new magazine aimed at a Northeastern suburb. The town was formerly a fairly classy venue, but it has inexorably been taken over (see the material on Prole Drift in the next chapter) by people who respond enthusiastically to rhetoric like this:

The greater——area represents a way of life. It is
a life-style. It is fine living...crystal for a special
dinner...a gourmet restaurant...the joy of a well-

written book. . . . It is life at its best . . . quiet
elegance . . . creative . . . beauty and grace. . . .
——*Magazine* will let you share in the dreams,
talents, contributions and achievements of a
community of people who stand apart from the
crowd and set high standards for themselves....
——*Magazine* is for intelligent, sensitive men,
women and children.——*Magazine* is you!

One could search widely without locating a more exemplary fusion of insecurity and snobbery, the one
propping up the other to produce that delicate equilib-
rium which sustains the middle class.

Cornball-elegant also is the rhetoric of the airlines
and of airports, whose clients are 90 percent middle-
class. If one couldn't infer the hopeless middle-classness of airports from their special understanding of the
ideas of *comfort*, *convenience*, and *lug-zhury*, one could
from their pretentious language, especially the way
they leap to designate themselves "International" or
even, like Houston, "Intercontinental." They will do
this on the slightest pretext, like having a plane take
off now and then for Acapulco or Alberta, while remaining utterly uncontaminated by any sign of internationalism, like dealing in foreign currencies or
speaking languages or sympathizing in any way with
international styles.

On the aircraft itself, virtually everything said or
written accords with the middle-class insistence that
words shall be bogus, from such formulations as "motion discomfort" and "flotation device" to "beverages"
and "non-dairy creamer." On a recent flight from New
York to London, a steward announced, "Smoking is
not permitted while you are making usage of the lav-
atory facilities"—a perfect example, almost a definition, of the middle-class pseudo-elegant style. The little
menu cards given out by transatlantic airlines, osten-

sibly to indicate the components of the meal but actually to tout the duty-free goods (including "designer" neckties and scarves), constitute a veritable exhibition palace of the fake elegant. One I've encountered on a TWA flight does forget itself and slip once, calling beverages *drinks* in a thoroughly upper-class way, but generally it holds the line, especially in describing the meals offered (I have added italics): "FILET TIPS DI-JONNAISE. Tidbits of Beef Tenderloin in a *Mild* Creamy Mustard Sauce *Presented with* Pommes Chateau and Petit Pois." Another meal is said to be "*Complemented by* Buttered Broccoli." And then, to cap it all: "Please accept our apologies if *due to previous passenger selections*, your *entree preference* is not available." Or, as a civilized person would put it, "Not all items available," the corollary of "No smoking in the toilets."

But *toilets* does not recommend itself to middle-class speakers, who prefer *lavatories* or *rest rooms*, euphemism as well as elegance being their hallmarks. One of their treasured possessions is a whole vocabulary of euphemized profanity and obscenity, so that when you hear "Holy Cow!" or "Holy Moses!" or hear that someone has done "a whale of a job," you know that a member of the middle class is nearby. It's hard to believe that after the numerous strains and scandals of the mid-twentieth century any relics survive of that class that used to say "O pshaw!" or "Botheration!" when it meant not just "O hell!" but "Shit!"—but we find the American Brigadier General Dozier, back home after weeks of bondage and humiliation at the hands of the most cruel and vicious Italian kidnappers, saying, "It's doggone good to be home." It's the middle class that insists still that *pregnant* be replaced by *expecting* or *starting a family (being in a family way*, on the other hand, is prole), and it has virtually legislated that all the rest of us *make love* instead of what we used to do. But in the face of all this the uppers stand firm. Jilly Cooper reports, "I once heard my son regaling his friends: 'Mummy says *pardon* is a much worse word than *fuck*.'" And of course the middle is where you hear false teeth called *dentures*, the rich called the *wealthy*, and dying called *passing away* (or *over*). (Proles are likely to be *taken to Jesus*.) Drunks are *people with alcohol problems*, the stupid are *slow learners* or *underachievers*, madness is *mental illness*, drug use is *drug abuse*, the crippled are *the handicapped* (sometimes, by a euphemism of a euphemism, *the challenged*), a slum is *the inner city*, and a graveyard is a *cemetery* or (among those more susceptible to advertising) *memorial park*. You can probably identify those sociologists who are firmly middle-class by their habit of calling proles *the supporting classes*. Discovering a few years ago that *sour* in the phrase "sweet and sour pork" conveyed bad associations to its middle-class clientele, your standard "Chinese" restaurant adjusted the language and came up with the safer "sweet and *pungent*" formula. Secure high-class people continue to say—indeed, insist upon saying—"sweet and sour"—a way of indicating that they've caught on to this dishonorable euphemistic act and disapprove of it vigorously. But the middle class, always delighted to accede to euphemisms whenever offered, and especially when offered by people selling anything, say "sweet and pungent," and feel good about it.

The middles cleave to euphemisms not just because they're an aid in avoiding facts. They like them also because they assist their social yearnings toward pomposity. This is possible because most euphemisms permit the speaker to multiply syllables, and the middle class confuses sheer numerousness with weight and value. Jonathan Swift amused himself by imagining spoken syllables as physical entities with "weight," density, specific gravity, and other purely physical attributes. The contemporary middle class acts as if embracing Swift's conception but without a trace of his irony. Thus instead of *now* it will say, weightily, *as of this time*, and instead of *later*, *subsequently*. It's like the middle-class trick of dressing up to go shopping. Hugh Rawson, in his invaluable *Dictionary of Euphemisms and Other Doubletalk* (1981), delivers the essential principle:

> *The longer the euphemism the better.* As a rule, . . . euphemisms are longer than the words they replace. They have more letters, they have more syllables, and frequently, two or more words will be deployed in place of a single one. This is partly because the tabooed Anglo-Saxon words tend to be short and partly because it almost always takes more words to evade an idea than to state it directly and honestly.

Rawson goes on to develop a nice pseudo-social-scientific "Fog or Pomposity Index," by which a euphemism's relation to the word or phrase it replaces can be quantified, high numbers indicating the greatest multiplication of syllables, or euphemisic success. Rawson's arithmetical details need not concern us. We can just note that the FOP Index of *prostitute* in relation to *whore* is 2.4, and in relation to *harlot*, 1.4. One of the highest FOP Indexes Rawson notes is earned by the designation *Personal Assistant to the Secretary (Special Activities)*, given to his *cook* by a former Cabinet member. This euphemism registers an FOP number of 17.8, which must be close to an all-time record.

So terrified of being judged socially insignificant is your typical member of the middle class, so ambitious of earning a reputation as a judicious thinker, indeed, almost an "executive," that it's virtually impossible for him to resist the temptation constantly to multiply syllables. He thus euphemizes willy-nilly. Indeed, it's sometimes hard to know whether the impulse to euphemize is causing the syllables to multiply, or whether the urge toward verbal weight and grandeur through multiplication is hustling the speaker into euphemism. The question confronts us when, inquiring what someone does, he answers not that he's a junk man, or even in the junk business, but in the scrap-iron business, or even the recycling business or reclamation industry. Occupational euphemisms always seem to entail multiplication of syllables. In many universities, what used to be the *bursar* is now the *disbursement officer*, just the way what used to be an *undertaker* (already sufficient as a euphemism, one would think) is now a *funeral director*, an advance of two whole syllables. (In raising *funeral director* to *grief therapist*, there's of course a loss of two syllables, but a compensating gain in "professionalism" and pseudo-medical pretentiousness.) *Selling* is raised to *retailing* or *marketing*, or even better, to *merchandising*, an act that exactly doubles its syllables, while *sales manager* in its turn is doubled by being raised to *Vice-President, Merchandising*. The person on the telephone who used to provide *Information* now gives (or more often, does not give) *Directory Assistance*, which is two syllables grander. Some sociologists surveying the status of occupations found that *druggist* ranked sixth out of fifteen. But when a syllable was added and the designation changed to *pharmacist*, the occupation moved up to fourth place.

Syllable multiplication usually occurs also in the euphemisms by which the middle class softens hard facts or cheerfulizes actuality. It's all in aid of avoiding anything "depressing." But you can aim for the verbally splendid at the same time. Thus *correctional facility* for *prison*, *work stoppage* or *industrial action* for *strike*, *discomfort* for *pain*, *homicide* for *murder*, *self-deliverance* for *suicide*, *fatality* for *death*. *Slum clearance* (three syllables) becomes *urban renewal* (five). *Nuclear device* has it over *atom bomb* both by a lot of euphemism and by two full syllables. Being by nature unmagnanimous (cf. Ronald Reagan), the middle class has always hated to tip, regarding it as a swindle, etc., but when you call a *tip* a *gratuity*, you take a little of the sting out.

The occasions when the middle class can, in its view, achieve high status by multiplying syllables are virtually infinite. Here we can list only a few examples. It is thought more impressive to say

cocktails	than	drinks
individuals	"	people
position	"	job
albeit	"	although
roadway	"	road
purchase	"	buy
conflagration	"	fire
billiard parlor	"	poolroom
launder	"	wash
affluent	"	rich (or "loaded")
currently	"	now
massive	"	big
meet with, or meet up with	"	meet
proceed	"	go
request	"	ask
subsequently	"	later
terminate	"	end
utilize	"	use
at the local level	"	locally

Sometimes this middle-class urge to add syllables propels the speaker toward grammar that is more prole than he might normally approve. Thus, sensing that *before* is a poor word compared with *previous*, he will say, "I had not been there previous." The motive is like that of the policeman at the Watergate hearings who, dissatisfied with the class standing of mere *went*, testified, "We then responded down the hall and into the office."

The passive voice is a great help to the middle class in multiplying syllables. Thus the TV newsman will say "No injuries were reported" (eight syllables) when he means "No one was hurt" (four). Pseudo-Latinism is another useful technique. *In colleges* has a measly four syllables, but *in academia* has six, just as *in the suburbs* has four but *in suburbia* five, and in addition conveys the suggestion that the speaker is familiar with the classical tongues. (A real Latinist would honor the

Proles say *TUX*, middles *TUXEDO*, but both are considered low by uppers, who say *DINNER JACKET* or (higher) *BLACK TIE*

accusative case and say *in suburbiam*, but let that pass.)
Another way of arriving at the goal of adding syllables
is simply to mistake one word for another, as the airline
steward did with *use* and *usage*. Thus the instructions
on a bottle of Calgon Floral Bouquet (formerly *bath
salts*) are headed, classily, *Usage Directions*. We can
infer the middle-class (rather than prole) origins of most
terrorist groups by their habit of leaving behind, after
their outrages, *communiqués* rather than *notes*, or even
messages. A benign, all-wise, and all-powerful editor
and supervisor of expression among the middle class
would have a busy time wielding his blue pencil. One
man asked by Coleman and Rainwater if he's better
off than his father answers yes, and explains: "I have
an M.A. and my father just finished high school. This
has meant that I am able to engage in higher-paying
areas of employment." Here the editor would strike
out all (twenty syllables) after *meant*, replacing those
words with the four syllables of *I can earn more*. The
ad for TV's *Brideshead Revisited* says, "This week
Sebastian's drinking problem grows worse." The kind
editor simply crosses out *problem*, and now the speaker's unfortunate middle-classhood is much less conspicuous.

Because, as De Tocqueville and Whitman were
aware, a special social anxiety is built into the American setup, this middle-class habit of adding syllables
lest one risk being unimpressive sometimes spreads
out and infects other classes. One can hear even fairly
classy people in the theater speaking not of *one-acts*
but of *one-acters*. We'll never know who conceived
that *vocalist* was a more impressive word than *singer*,
but now regardless of class any American is likely to
ask, "Who's the vocalist on that record?" On the ped-
iment of the Supreme Court building are the words
EQUAL JUSTICE UNDER LAW. In *Washington Itself*

(1981), E. J. Applewhite points out that people secure in their reputation for seriousness, wisdom, and social adequacy would not have multiplied syllables but inscribed simply JUSTICE, having scrutinized the five extra syllables and perceived that all were implied in that one simple word. But being Americans, they were afraid someone would find them elemental and modest and thus socially unsatisfactory unless they canted it up.

Before turning to a closer examination of the special idiom of the proles, we should note a few more middle-class signals. An excessive fondness for metaphors is one, things like grinding to a halt or running the gamut or boggling the mind, which are never recognized as clichés, and indeed, if they were so recognized, would be treasured all the more. Middle-class speakers are also abnormally fond of acronyms (Mothers United for Fiduciary Security: MUFFS), certainly as an exclusionary mechanism to keep the uninitiated and the impure (i.e., the proles) at a distance, but also as an inclusionary device, to solidify the in-group or corporate or team consciousness (cf. "officers' wives") without which the middle class flies all apart. Although the middles don't quite use such expressions as *milady* and *mine host*, advertisers understand that when such expressions are aimed at them, they will not gag. The middle class likewise thinks quite elegant the expression (corporate?) *over* drinks (or *over* coffee or *over* dinner) rather than *with* or *at*: "Let's discuss it over drinks." (It's the impulse toward metaphor again—fancier than the literal.) The classes not anxious about their own sophistication would more likely say, "Let's have a drink and talk about it." A similar impulse to splendor motivates the middle class to inscribe "Regrets Only" on their social invitations, where the more unpretending classes would say "No's Only," a way of implying less about the implicit desirability of the party. As middles grow worse educated, they tend to employ more pretentious, pseudo-scientific terms to dignify the ordinary or to suggest noble purpose in normal or commonplace behavior: the word *parenting* is an example. Saying *parenting* is virtually the equivalent of telling us on your bumper that you always brake for small animals.

When we hear speakers entirely careless of the former distinction between *less* and *fewer* ("Less white prisoners are in our penal institutions today....") or bothering to add the *is concerned* or *goes* to the phrase *as far as* ("as far as the Republican Party..."), we know we're approaching the idiomatic world identifiable as prole. Proles signal their identity partly by pronunciation, like the Texan on the Buckley show who said *pro-mís-kitty* and "I am a prole" at the same time. Proles drop the *g* on present participles, saying *it's a fuckin' shame*, as well as the *-ed* on past participles: thus *corned beef* becomes *corn beef* (or better, *corm beef*), and we hear also of *bottle beer*, *dark-skin people*, *old-fashion bake beans*, and *Mother's High-Power Beer*. "First come, first serve" is a favorite axiom. Roger Price, the student of Roobs or urban hicks, has located more prole pronunciations. He observes that "in Southern California even newscasters say 'wunnerful' and 'anna-bi-od-dicks' and 'in-er*ess*-ting.' The word 'interesting,' pronounced in this manner, with the accent on the third syllable, is the infallible mark of the Roob." Or, as we call it, the prole. To Price other signs of Roobhood are saying

fack	for	fact
fure	"	fewer
present	"	president
oney	"	only

| finey | for | finally, and |
| innaleckshul | " | "nondemocratic" |

To say *én-tire*, like the Rev. Rex Humbard, the TV evangelist, is to indicate that you're a high or mid-prole, but to say *merring-gew* when you mean the foamy egg-white stuff on top of pies is low.

Proles of all types have terrible trouble with the apostrophe, and its final disappearance from English, which seems imminent, will be a powerful indication that the proles have won. "Modern Cabinet's," announces a sign in the Middle West, comparable to its Eastern counterpart, "Rutger's Electrical Supply Company." Sometimes the apostrophe simply vanishes, as in *Ladies Toilet*. But then, as if the little mark were, somehow, missed, it, or something like it, is invoked anomalously as if its function were like underlining:

> Your Driver: 'Tom Bedricki'
> 'Today's Specials'
> 'Tipping Permitted'

Proles like to use words that normally appear only in newspapers. They don't realize that no one *calls* the Pope *the pontiff* except in pretentious journalese, or a senator *a lawmaker*, or the United States *the nation*, or a scholar *an educator*. This last is not objected to by high-school teachers and administrators, who rather embrace it as an elevating professional euphemism. Thus it's purely for social-class reasons that university professors object to being denominated *educators*, because the term fails to distinguish them from high-school superintendents, illiterate young teachers with temporary "credentials," and similar pedagogic riffraff. The next time you meet a distinguished university professor, especially one who fancies himself well known nationally for his ideas and writings, tell him it's an honor to meet such a famous educator, and watch: first he will look down for a while, then up, but not at you, then away. And very soon he will detach himself from your company. He will be smiling all the time, but inside he will be in torment.

Prole fondness for newspaper words tempts them into some extravagant malapropisms. A writer in the London *Sunday Times* not long ago testified to hearing that attempts were being made to *pervert* a strike, and that somewhere a priest had been called in to *circumcise* a ghost:

> Readers notify me of the lady with a painful "Ulster" in her mouth; the shrines you can see in Catholic countries in commemoration of "St. Mary Mandolin"; the police at the scene of a crime, who threw "an accordion" round the street; the touching sight of the deceased George V lying in state on a "catapult" . . . the student who was always to be found "embossed" in a book; the pilot who left his aircraft by means of the "ejaculation seat"; . . . the drowning swimmer who was revived by means of "artifical insemination"; and the rainbow which was said by an onlooker to contain "all the colors of the rectum."

You're likely to hear from high-prole speakers the word *penultimate* used to mean absolutely the last, or absolutely the most, as in "Nuclear weapons are the penultimate threat." A serious moment in cultural history occurred a few years ago, marking a significant takeover of public rhetoric by proles. I'm referring to gasoline trucks changing the warning word on the rear from INFLAMMABLE to FLAMMABLE. Widespread public education had at last produced a population which no longer recognized *in-* as an intensifier. The proles for whom the sign FLAMMABLE was devised will be impelled when they hear that something (like a book or a work of art) is *invaluable* to toss it into the trash immediately. The rhetorical situation grows funny when prole ignorance of *inflammable* joins with middle-class pretentiousness to produce an artifact like this label on a bath mat: "Flammable ... Should not be used near sources of ignition." The author of this presumably imagines that slow learners so dull as to require *flammable* will be able to figure out that *sources of ignition* means fire.

If unexpected silence is one sign of the upper classes (necessary, for example, as Nancy Mitford notes, after someone has said, on departing, "It was so nice seeing you"), noise and vociferation identify the proles, who shout "Wahoo!" at triumphant moments in games (largely hockey and pro football) they attend. Speaking to Studs Terkel, a Chicago policeman (high-prole, probably) indicates his awareness of one important distinction between his class and those below. "If my mother and father argued," he reports, "my mother went around shutting down the windows because they didn't want the neighbors to hear 'em. But they [i.e., the lower sort of proles] deliberately open the doors and open the windows, screaming and hollering...." The prole must register his existence and his presence in public. Thus the conversations designed to be overheard (and admired) in public conveyances, and the prole way of humming tunes audibly, as if hoping to be complimented on pitch, tempo, or attack. The middle class, fearing ridicule or social failure, doesn't do these things: it leaves them to proles, who are not going anywhere. Noise is a form of overstatement, and one reason the upper orders still regard selling anything as rather vulgar is that the art of moving merchandise is so dependent on overstatement. Thus minimal utterance is high-class, while proles say everything two or three times. "Ummmmm" is a frequently heard complete sentence among the uppers.

By what other language signs are proles to be known? By their innocence of the objective case, for one thing. Recalling vaguely that it is polite to mention oneself last, as in "He and I were there," proles apply this principle uniformly and come up with "Between he and I." There's also a prole problem with *like*. Proles remember being told something by middle-class schoolmarms about the dangers of illiteracy the use of *like* invites, but not being able to remember exactly, they hope to stay out of trouble by always using *as* instead. They finally say things like "He looks as his father." Another prole signal is difficulty with the complex sentence, resulting in structures displaying elaborate pseudo-"correct" participles like "Being that it was a cold day, the furnace was on." Because the gerund is beyond their reach, they are forced to multiply words (always a pleasure, really) and say, "The people in front of him at the show got mad due to the fact that he talked so much" instead of "His talking at the show annoyed the people in front." (*People*, however, is not quite right: *individuals* is more likely.) Just as the prole dimly recalls a problem with *like*, he also remembers something about *lying* and *laying*. But what? Because he can't recall, he simplifies his problem and uses *laying* for everything. People thus *lay* on the beach, the bed, the grass, and the sidewalk, without necessarily any suggestion that they're engaged in sexual performances. And there's a final prole stigma. Proles adore being called "*Mr.* [First Name] Prole." Thus proles who have made it to celebrated stations in life are customarily addressed or referred to in public by that title, no matter how inappropriate it may seem to the sophisticated. Thus we hear of "Mr. Frank Sinatra" and "Mr. Howard Cosell." And on the radio: "Ladies and Gentlemen, [portentous pause], Mr. Frank Perdue."

If each class has one word it responds to uniquely, the upper class probably likes *secure* or *liquid* best. The word of the upper-middle class is *right*, as in doing the right thing: "I do want everything right for Muffy's wedding." The middle class likes *right* too, but the word that really excites the middles is *luxury* ("Those beautiful luxury one-room apartments"). *Spotless* (floors, linens, bowels, etc.) is also a middle-class favorite. High proles are suckers for *easy*—easy terms, six easy lessons. And the word of the classes below is *free*: "We never go to anything that's not free," as the low-prole housewife said.

A very little attention to the different idioms of the classes should persuade the most sentimental not only that there is a tight system of social class in this country but that linguistic class lines are crossed only rarely and with great difficulty. A virtually bottomless social gulf opens between those who say "Have a nice day" and those who say, on the other hand, "Goodbye," those who when introduced say "Pleased to meet you" and those who say "How do you do?" There may be some passing intimacy between those who think *momentarily* means *in a moment* (airline captain over loudspeaker: "We'll be taking off momentarily, folks") and those who know it means *for a moment*, but it won't survive much strain. It's like the tenuous relation between people who conceive that *type* is an adjective ("She's a very classy type person") and people who know it's only a noun or verb. The sad thing is that by the time one's an adult, these stigmata are virtually unalterable and ineffaceable. We're pretty well stuck for life in the class we're raised in. Even adopting all the suggestions implied in this chapter, embracing all the high-class locutions and abjuring the low ones, won't help much.

CLIMBING AND SINKING, AND PROLE DRIFT

THE DIFFICULTY OF CHANGING CLASS DETERS THE millions trying to ascend as little as the thousands trying to sink, and it would be sad to calculate the energy wasted in both pursuits. "Strainers" rather than "climbers" is the name the sociologist August B. Hollingshead gives those who try to move upward without in any way making it. Among the strainers, we can gather, are the clients of Rozanne Weissman, a Washington, D.C., status therapist, who instructs the ambitious there in the technique of social climbing. She advises aspirants to get their names into local gossip columns with the expectation that invitations to embassy parties will ensue. That is pitiable, embassy parties being close to the very social bottom. Outright lying is sometimes useful, if only temporarily, to the class climber. One janitor says: "When you meet somebody at a party they ask, 'What do you do?' I bullshit them. I tell 'em anything. . . . 'I'm a CPA.'"

Some of the most assiduous class climbers are university professors. C. Wright Mills has their number: "Men can achieve position in this field," he perceives, "although they are recruited from the lower-middle class, a milieu not remarkable for grace of mind, flexibility or breadth of culture, or scope of imagination. The profession thus includes many persons who have experienced a definite rise in class and status position, and who in making the climb are more likely . . . to have acquired 'the intellectual than the social graces.' It also includes people of 'typically plebeian cultural interests outside the field of specialization, and a generally philistine style of life.'" Thus the deep instinct of the professor to go bowling, although another part of him will tug upward, dragging him toward costly summers among persons of inherited money at the most solid resorts.

The mail-order catalogs we've looked at do a lot of business with middle-class people who aspire to rise but whose circumstances enable them to do so only in fantasy. By buying items like a T-shirt reading "Preppy Drinking Shirt," the middles can persuade themselves that they're sending up their own upper-middle tradition rather than hankering after a status they're never really going to achieve. (The actual audience for this Preppy Drinking Shirt is all too plainly indicated by such other items offered in the same catalog as a musical dustpan, which, when deployed, plays "Born Free"; and "The World's Smallest Harmonica.") Fantasist class climbers are well served by another mail-order firm which offers a nine-by-twelve-foot wallpaper panel, a photographic mural in deep, rich browns, depicting a doorway with adjoining bookcases in an upper-class library: the floors are parquet, the cabinetwork hardwood, the books bound in leather, and there's lots of molding around the impressive, wide double doorway. You stick this up on your middle-class wall—"Goes on like wallpaper"—and every time you view it, especially if you squint your eyes a bit or are slightly drunk, you can imagine your class rising gratifyingly.

If social climbing, whether in actuality or in fantasy, is well understood, social sinking is not, although there's more of it going on than most people notice. Male homosexuals and lesbians, respectively, exemplify these two opposite maneuvers. Ambitious male homosexuals, at least in fantasy, aspire to rise, and from humble origins to ascend to the ownership of antique businesses, art galleries, and hair salons. The object is to end by frequenting the Great. They learn to affect elegant telephone voices and gravitate instinctively toward "style" and the grand. Lesbians, on the contrary, like to sink, dropping from middle-class status to become taxi drivers, police officers, and construction workers. The ultimate male-homosexual social dream is to sit at an elegant dinner table, complete with flowers and doilies and finger bowls, surrounded by rich, successful, superbly suited and gowned, witty, and cleverly immoral people. The ultimate lesbian social dream is to pack it in at some matey lunch counter with the heftier proles, wearing work clothes and doing a lot of shouting and kidding.

Like lesbians, men of letters sometimes display an inordinate desire to sink in class. There's T. E. Lawrence entering the RAF as a ranker and Norman Mailer allying himself with the murderous prole Jack Henry Abbott. Are they motivated by guilt over the advantages their classy educations have given them? Drinking too much is a standard mechanism for class sinking, as a glance at the Bowery will confirm, and since authors traditionally are drinkers, we'd expect many to solicit a drop in class by that means. Writers and the sophisticated also try to sink by affecting the garb of the prole classes, like Ivy students who wear housepainters' overalls or join communes. Or they will dress like the low-status young, becoming what Leslie Fiedler has called "teenage impersonators." But the idea is seldom to sink just one class. To sink successfully, if you are upper-middle or middle, you have to sink deep. But as few sink successfully as rise credibly. No matter how much effort you expend, if your language doesn't give you away, your grammar will, or your taste in clothes or cars or ideas. The upper-class person caught slumming is as worthy of the scorn of proles for not dropping his *g*'s as the prole among the upper classes betrayed by revealing that he has no idea how to eat an artichoke. Of course, much social sinking is not at all intentional. Inflation, unemployment, a static economy, and lowered productivity have made all too apparent what Paul Blumberg calls "the Europeani-zation of the American class system," which means "a more rigid structure and greater inequality." After de-cades of moving up, "the mass of Americans now find themselves... *bumped down*." There used to be room at the top. Now, says Blumberg, "there... seems om-inously to be ample room at the bottom."

In a melancholy sense, the whole society could be said to be engaged in a process of class sinking. Prole Drift, we can call it, a term that will suggest the ten-dency in advanced industrialized societies for every-thing inexorably to become proletarianized. Prole drift seems an inevitable attendant of mass production, mass selling, mass communication, and mass education, and some of its symptoms are best-seller lists, films that must appeal to virtually everyone (except the intelli-gent, sensitive, and subtle), shopping malls, and the lemming flight to the intellectual and cultural emptiness of the Sun Belt. Prole drift is another term for what Blumberg calls the Howard Johnsonization of Amer-ica. "The characteristic of the hour," says Ortega y Gasset in *The Revolt of the Masses* (1930), "is that the commonplace mind, knowing itself to be common-

commonplace and to impose them wherever it will."
As a result of this process, the wine of life, as Donald
Barthelme notes, turns into Gatorade, a redaction for
a later time of Ezra Pound's earlier observation that
the pianola is rapidly replacing Sappho's barbitos. Prole
drift is what they're all talking about.

Evidence of prole drift is everywhere. Look at magazines and newspapers. Serious historical students of
prole drift would find significant the disappearance
during the 1940s of the table of contents from the front
cover of *The Atlantic* and its replacement by a "picture." Why did this happen? A close critic could infer
only that the former audience for language was dying
off or going blind with senility and not at all being
reconstituted in the old way by the newly educated.
More evidence of prole drift is to be found by looking
at newspaper features. The anthropologist Marcello
Truzzi, examining this country's newspapers in 1972,
found that while twenty years earlier only about 100
of the 1,750 daily papers carried astrological columns,
now 1,200 did. Or look at the ads in *The New Republic*,
formerly a magazine whose audience was thought, even
by advertisers, to consist of liberals, skeptics, atheists,
intellectuals, and programmatic nay-sayers. Here's an
ad that appeared in 1982:

REVEREND PHYLLIS MICHELE

Past   Present   Future

ASTROLOGY   TAROT   PSYCHOMETRY

3 Questions—$10

"High Degree of Accuracy."

Another ad aimed at the "new" *New Republic* readers assumes that, presumably because they've passed through an American high school, they are incompetent at simple arithmetical procedures. For them, an indispensable crutch, a

---

TIPPER'S TABLE. Wallet-size card for figuring 15% tips. $1.00. Rithmetics, Box 720, Tillamook, OR.

The drift of the *New York Times* audience prolewards assumed by advertisers there is to be gauged from a recent expensive quarter-page ad. This was getting off an "American Eagle Commemorative Belt Buckle," in silver plate, depicting an eagle against a mountain background, the sort of artifact normally appealing only to a shabby dude cowboy or adolescent youth. "These buckles," said the ad, "will be minted in a strictly limited edition" and for one year only, "after which time the dies will be permanently destroyed." This will easily be recognized as the sort of con that formerly would have found its audience among the readers of *Popular Mechanics*, naturally susceptible to the come-on of "collectibles." Now it is addressed, and we must imagine with considerable effectiveness, business being business, to an audience of brokers, foundation executives, university presidents, scholars, physicians, and attorneys. Prole drift is hardly better illustrated, except by an announcement which appeared only four days after the *Times* belt-buckle scandal, this one in the formerly sacrosanct London *Times Literary Supplement*. This weekly used to be virtually identical with ideas of rhetorical meticulousness and verbal class. But look at it now:

READERS OF TIMES LITERARY SUPPLEMENT
INCLUDE PUBLISHERS, ACADEMICS AND
THOSE INVOLVED IN
THE LITERARY WORLD.

So far, not bad, despite the illiterate omission of THE before TIMES. That oversight we might impute to a printer's error, but not what follows:

> It is, therefore, an ideal media in which to advertise your senior management and editorial vacancies.

Similar evidence of prole drift will confront you the minute you inquire into what has happened at your local bookstore. It's not so much that it now sells calendars and posters of funny cats and greeting cards and paper toys. It's that in its vending of books it perfectly illustrates Roger Price's First Law: "If everybody doesn't want it, nobody gets it." You used to be able freely to order any book in print and pick it up at the bookstore within a week or so. No longer. Now it's such a big deal that all but the most pushy will refrain from this behavior. Chain bookstores—are there now any others?—not only charge a $2 fee for orders now but often require a deposit of half the price of the book. These impediments they try to rationalize by renaming what used to be *orders*: to emphasize the rarity and difficulty of this procedure, they now call them *special orders*. This makes them sound very outré and difficult, indeed, all but impossible. The effect of this is clear. Customers will be encouraged to cleave rigidly to the best-seller list, permitting themselves an interest only in things which the bookstore manager (formerly, *bookseller*) has thought it profitable to order in quantity. The customer will quickly learn that he should never be so foolish as to walk into a bookstore and say something like "Have you a copy of Matthew Arnold's *Culture and Anarchy*?" or "Do you have Freud's *Civilization and Its Discontents*?" Why be curious about commodities like these when stacks of Leon Uris and Ann Landers are all conveniently laid out before you? Further evidence of prole drift in the book world is the replacement of the National Book Awards by the American Book Awards, so cunningly similar in name, so totally different in import. Where the National Book Awards used to signal critical merit, being determined by disinterested and intellectually impressive judges, the American simulacra, determined now by publishers and editors, advertising and merchandising people and bookstore employees, recognize not a book's excellence but its popularity and sales potential. These two novelties, the new bookstore practice with "special orders" and the commercialization of the book awards, may seem small things, but intellectually they are close to a national disaster, an illustration right around the corner from where you live of Ortega's gloomy finding that "the mass crushes beneath it everything that is different, everything that is excellent, individual, qualified, and select." Which is a way of saying that proles, who superficially look like losers, have a way of always winning. For Ortega, writing in 1930, the emergent prole was a "vertical invader," pushing his way up to contaminate a heretofore sacrosanct domain of art, culture, complexity, and subtlety. Time, however, has shown that the prole is staying right where he is and is not invading anything. Rather, the world on top is sinking down to fit itself to his wants, since purchasing power has increasingly concentrated itself in his hands.

Further evidence of prole drift (if more is really needed) is the behavior of customers in stores and

markets and banks and post offices. Queuing—whether
in Eastern Europe or the Free World an infallible signal
of proletarianization—is now commonplace everywhere, and the supine clients wait with animal-like
patience while the clerk interrupts proceedings to chat
with friends on the phone or simply disappears for long
periods. And why not? The customer, quite used to
conceiving of himself as a slave and a nonentity, never
complains. No one objects when a retail transaction
takes three times longer than it did ten years ago because now it's enacted on a computerized cash register. The more normal, necessary, and acceptable the
delay seems, the more proletarianized you know we've
become. Normal and acceptable also is the disappearance of service and amenity everywhere, the virtual
universality of "self-service" (as if it were a good thing)
in stores and outlets of all kinds. Self-service is *ipso
facto* prole. Proles like it because it minimizes the risk
of social contact with people who might patronize or
humiliate them. All right for them, but because of prole
drift we're all obliged to act as if we were hangdog no-
accounts.

There used to be different audiences for different
things. Those who went to see *My Fair Lady* were not
the people who liked to watch, on TV, *Diff'rent Strokes*.
But now Broadway musicals routinely advertise on TV
as if the two audiences were identical, and producers
of musicals solicit for their product the audience which
is the avowed enemy of wit, nuance, subtlety, and
style. The musical *Forty-second Street* is so devoid of
anything but the most prole stereotypes that it naturally
attracts the same viewers as *Three's Company* or *The
Love Boat*, as its producers revealed by advertising it
extensively on television.

A related sign of prole drift (or rather, precipitate
lunge) is the current replacement of two good tradi-

tional New York theaters by one bad New York hotel. This operation, which took place in the spring of 1982, coincided with the announcement by the maker of the Checker Cab that he was discontinuing production of this vehicle, the only civilized taxi available in the United States. At the same time American brewers made public what the more sensitive wits have known for years—that prole drift is grossly apparent in American beer. The brewers noted that they have greatly reduced the hop content, because hops give beer taste and bitterness. Proles want blah and sweetness, and thus, as a brewing spokesman says, "The level of bitterness in American beers has decreased in the last ten years by maybe 20 percent and the whole flavor level has come down." That's the beer you and I have to drink, friend, and there's no escape except emigration. Or having enough money always to consume beer brought in from Germany or Holland.

THE BRICK BOX: ONE MODEL FITS ALL

It may not yet be quite true that, as Auden puts it,

> Intellectual disgrace
> Stares from every human face,

but it seems the more true the more you meditate on the proletarianization of architecture since the Second World War. Now, the same rectangular brick box will do for a church, a school, a hospital, a prison, a dormitory, a motel, a fire station, or a business building. The implicit point this universal brick box makes is not merely that no one's interested in fine distinctions between functions. It's that no one's interested in distinctions at all. And of course the use of civilized allusion in public architecture disappeared some time ago. Now you can look in vain for acorns, wreaths, balustrades, finials, metopes and triglyphs—all the decorations that used to point to a world larger than the local and a purpose nobler than the utilitarian. The sad thing is that we do get what we deserve. Societies in the grip of prole drift may expect prole architecture, a point nicely developed in Kingsley Amis's "Aberdarcy: The Main Square":

> By the new Boots, a tool-chest with flagpoles
> Glued on, and flanges, and a dirty great
> Baronial doorway, and things like portholes,
> Evans met Mrs Rhys on their first date.
>
> Beau Nash House, that sells Clothes for Gentlemen,
> Jacobethan, every beam nailed on tight—
> Real wood, though, mind you—was in full view when
> Lunching at the Three Lamps, she said all right.
>
> And he dropped her beside the grimy hunk
> Of castle, that with luck might one day fall
> On to the *Evening Post*, the time they slunk
> Back from that lousy week-end in Porthcawl.
>
> The journal of some bunch of architects
> Named this the worst town centre they could find;

But how disparage what so well reflects
Permanent tendencies of heart and mind?

All love demands a witness: something "there"
Which it yet makes part of itself. These two
Might find Carlton House Terrace, St Mark's
    Square,
A bit on the grand side. What about you?

ᚷ[IX]ᚷ

THE X WAY OUT

WHAT ABOUT US, INDEED? WHAT CLASS ARE WE IN, and what do we think about our entrapment there? A useful exercise is to ask of Amis's poem, what class is the speaker in it? Not a prole, we know, because his grammar is unexceptionable. Not middle-class either, because he notices that something's deeply wrong with the public architecture of Aberdarcy and has no fear of starting controversy by criticizing it. And he can't be upper-class because he's speaking in verse, which requires talent, learning, and effort. His sharp eye, satiric humor, and complex comic sympathy for poor middle-class Evans and Mrs. Rhys, in addition to his artistic sensitivity, suggest a special identity. Let's say that the speaker is not in a class at all but is rather a member of category X.

"X" people are better conceived as belonging to a category than a class because you are not born an X person, as you are born and reared a prole or a middle. You become an X person, or, to put it more bluntly, you earn X-personhood by a strenuous effort of discovery in which curiosity and originality are indispensable. And in discovering that you can become an X person you find the only escape from class. Entering category X often requires flight from parents and forebears. The young flocking to the cities to devote themselves to "art," "writing," "creative work"—anything, virtually, that liberates them from the presence of a boss or supervisor—are aspirant X people, and if they succeed in capitalizing on their talents, they may end as fully fledged X types.

What kind of people are Xs? The old-fashioned term *bohemians* gives some idea; so does the term *the talented*. Some Xs are intellectuals, but a lot are not: they are actors, musicians, artists, sports stars, "celebrities," well-to-do former hippies, confirmed residers abroad, and the more gifted journalists, those whose by-lines intelligent readers recognize with pleasant anticipation. X people can be described as (to use C. Wright Mills's term) "self-cultivated." They tend to be self-employed, doing what social scientists call autonomous work. If, as Mills has said, the middle-class person is "always somebody's man," the X person is nobody's, and his freedom from supervision is one of his most obvious characteristics. X people are independent-minded, free of anxious regard for popular shibboleths, loose in carriage and demeanor. They adore the work they do, and they do it until they are finally carried out, "retirement" being a concept meaningful only to hired personnel or wage slaves who despise their work. Being an X person is like having much of the freedom and some of the power of a top-out-of-sight or upper-class person, but without the money. X category is a sort of unmonied aristocracy.

Identifying X people is not difficult once you know the signs. Their dress and looks, for one thing. Since there's no one they think worth impressing by mere appearance, X people tend to dress for themselves alone, which means they dress comfortably, and generally "down." One degree down will usually do the trick: if black tie is designated, an X person appears in a dark suit (of a distinctly unstylish, archaic cut) and a notable necktie. If suits are expected, he omits the tie. If "informal" is the proclaimed style, his jeans will be torn and patched, his cords very used, if not soiled. If others are wearing bathing suits, X people are likely to show up naked. X shoes are always comfortable, regardless of current modes, and they usually suggest that they have been chosen (like sandals and moccasins) for walking on soft carpets of pine needles. Indeed, L. L. Bean and Land's End are the main costumers for X people, who annually consume the bulk of the down vests, flannel shirts, and hiking boots vended in this country. Xs are likely to wear these things specifically where most people are got up in jackets and nice dresses. If the Xs ever descend to legible clothing, the words—unlike BUDWEISER or U.S.A. DRINKING TEAM—are original and interesting, although no comment on them is ever expected. Indeed, visibly to notice them would be bad form. When an X person, male or female, meets a member of an identifiable class, the costume, no matter what it is, conveys the message "I am freer and less terrified than you are," or—in extreme circumstances—"I am more intelligent and interesting than you are: please do not bore me." The question of whether to select a black or a beige raincoat never troubles X people, for they don't use raincoats at all: they either get wet and pay no attention or wait under cover—they are not the slaves of timeclocks—until the rain stops. X people are almost never fat, for they exercise a lot, naturally and for the fun of it. They were exercising thirty years ago, before the upper-middles had been instructed about jogging by the popular press. Favorite X sport: ad hoc games of touch football, especially while slightly drunk. X people tend to eschew the obvious kinds of pets, leaning instead toward things like tame coyotes, skunks, peacocks, and anteaters. X people are likely to appear with unexplained sexual partners, and some have been known to become pregnant at socially inappropriate moments. Their infant issue they may tote about in ways that appear novel, if not shocking, to the middle class: in slings, for example, or backpack papoose carriers.

The places where X people choose to live usually have a decent delicatessen and a good wine store. There is likely to be a nearby Army and Navy or hiking shop, for the dress-down clothes, and a good public or university library as a stay against boredom. A sophisticated newsdealer is also an attraction, for one needs British, French, German, and Italian periodicals. X people move away when they, not their bosses, feel they should. They like where they live, and when they stop liking their location—when, for example, it seems drifting too speedily middle- or prolewards—they move. Their houses, which are never positioned in "developments," tend to be sited oddly—on the sides of mountains, say, or planted stubbornly between skyscrapers. Their houses (never, of course, "homes") are more likely to be old than new: old ones are cheaper, for one thing, and by flaunting a well-used house you can proclaim your freedom from the childish American obsession with the up-to-date. Since X people disdain the standard kinds of status display, their houses are likely to have no driveways, and their cars, unstylish and most often unwashed, will be parked in the street. The understatement principle governing the kind and condition of the automobile will determine that no stickers, college or any other kind, ever appear in the windows, although a black-and-white "A" sticker, indicating the minimal gasoline ration during the Second

World War, would be a permissible archaic gesture. Of course X people shun turnpikes and freeways, those tedious, characterless conduits for the middle class, preferring instead slowpoke back roads because of their "charm." In the X spirit of parody, the lawn and yard of the X house are never impressive and often give off powerful satiric overtones. Thus instead of grass the front yard may feature a spread of gravel, asphalt, or cement (sometimes painted bright green), haphazard arrangements of stones and weeds, and ostentatious marijuana patches. In addition to parody middle-class effects, parody prole items may make an appearance, like ironically ugly lawn furniture and joke flower-bed edgings. But regardless of the way it's furnished, the front yard must be nondescript, for the street façade of the house is negligible to Xs, the backyard being the important place because private. There you can play unobserved. X people like to have houseguests, although they never designate them by that upper-middle-class term. They lodge them not in guest rooms but on spare couches or in sleeping bags, and there may be lots of coming and going at night, never mentioned in the morning.

The readiest way to describe an X living room is to say that anything recommended in a sound home-furnishings magazine will not appear there. The guiding principle will be parody display: there may be an elephant's foot umbrella stand and some unlikely manifestations of the art of the taxidermist—stuffed cats and dogs, penguins, iguanas. Lots of campy fabric—odd curtains, fringed shawls draped about, walls covered in museum cloth. The pictures on the walls will bespeak vigorous inner-directedness: there will be shameless nudes (all sexes and ages), and instead of the chart of Nantucket or Catalina Island favored by the upper-middles, a chart of Bikini Atoll or Guadalcanal. On the coffee table, *Mother Jones* and *Bulletin of the Atomic Scientists*. The nearer you approach pure X the closer to the floor you find yourself sitting. The ultimate X living room displays no furniture legs at all, no sitting, dining, or reclining surface being higher than twelve inches from the floor. The floor is either entirely bare wood or covered irregularly with thick rugs, always from uncommon places like Nepal or Honduras. There will usually be a large and not too neat working fireplace, less because it's pretty than because it's fun to copulate on the floor in front of it. And there are copious bookshelves packed with hardbound books, most of them dating from well before the 1950s.

X people watch a lot of TV but never look at anything remotely improving, regarding National Educational Television as a menace to culture. On their sets, which will often display a fairground plaster Popeye on top, Xs like to watch classic reruns like *The Honeymooners* and *I Love Lucy*, experiencing ecstasies watching for the fiftieth time Jackie Gleason's Chef of the Future or Lucy's manic game of golf. By these pursuits X people pay their own obeisance to the great status principle of archaism. They will often seek out live transmissions, in the hope of witnessing comic error—the football flubbed, the manuscript of the public speech blown away and scattered by an impudent gust, the gaffe extempore committed by a President, governor, senator, mayor, or high clergyman. X people still treasure the moment during John F. Kennedy's inauguration when the speaker's stand being used for public prayer by His Eminence Richard Cardinal Cushing suddenly caught fire, the ominous wisps of smoke unperceived by the unwitting grandees on the platform.

Drinking: X people drink not to show off but to get quietly tight. Vodka and gin they find the most expedient means to this end, although some Xs will also be seen drinking white wine pretty freely. Regardless of the tipple, X people like to buy it in quantity and cheaply, specializing in excellent but unknown liquor-store house brands—Beefeater Gin and Cutty Sark Scotch betray the credulous victim of advertising, and hence the middle class—and on X premises gallon jugs of drink are commonly seen.

X people seldom eat at stated mealtimes, hunger and convenience being their only motivations for eating. Like the uppers, Xs generally eat late rather than early, and their meals tend to last a long time, what with all the prolonged comic and scandalous narrative at table. The X cuisine is seldom the pseudo-French or mock-British of the upper-middle class: it is more likely to be North African, or Turkish, or "Indo-Chinese," or vegetarian, or "organic," or "health." Feeling no insecure need to display themselves in the act of dominating inferiors by issuing orders and demanding that their whims be honored, X people generally avoid eating out. Intelligent and perceptive as they are, they know that if you're at all clever, you can feed better at home. Besides, Xs go in for a lot of things you can't readily get out, like herbal teas, lemon-flavored vodka, and baked goods made of stone-ground flour. Now and then X people will suddenly, without warning, lurch away from their usual exotic foods and go ape American, eating nothing but apple pies, hams, hot dogs, hamburgers, chili, and turkey. But regardless of the style of the cuisine, X food is always (1) good and (2) unpraised by the company, its excellence taken for granted. Except for the occasional sauterne or after-dinner port, the wine is dry, good, and never discussed. There's one surefire way, other things being equal, to identify an X dinner party. All the wine brought by guests, no matter the quantity, is inevitably consumed, and so is more of the host's stock than he's probably anticipated.

Instinctively unprovincial, X people tend to be unostentatiously familiar with the street layouts and landmarks of London, Paris, and Rome—and sometimes Istanbul and Karachi. This is in accord with their habit of knowing a lot for the pleasure of it, as well as their more specific curiosity about people, no matter where or when they live. Hence the X interest in history, literature, architecture, and aesthetic styles. (The critic of Aberdarcy's main square is right in the center of the tradition.) Regardless of the work they do, the Xs read a great deal, and they regard reading as a normal part of experience, as vital as "experience" and often more interesting. They never belong to book clubs. Because they choose their own books entirely themselves, they will often be heard complaining about the vulgarity and hopelessness of their local book outlets. The X reader reads everything, his curiosity being without limit. On occasion he will even read best-sellers, but largely to see if their cliché content is as high as usual. X people have usually "been to college," but they generally throw out unread, together with other junk mail, their college alumni magazine.

Being entirely self-directed, X people pursue remote and uncommonplace knowledge—they may be fanatical about Serbo-Croatian prosody, geodes, or Northern French church vestments of the eleventh century. When in a flux of joy X people burst into song, the air is likely to derive from opera of the Baroque period, or from *Don Giovanni* or *The Messiah*. Even the tunes they whistle will be from the classical repertory: a really able X person can whistle a given Beethoven quarter with hardly a lapse. X people are good at playing musical instruments, but seldom the expected ones: instead of the violin or the recorder, they will play the melophone, the autoharp, or the nose flute.

Although X people abjure the word *creative*, regarding it as stylish, sentimental, psychologically naive, and therefore middle-class, they adopt toward cultural objects the attitude of makers, and of course critics. It's not hard for an X person to imagine himself producing any contemporary work of art or drama or architecture. Thus with films X people are as interested in the styles of directors as of actors. Although they may know a great deal about European ecclesiastical architecture and even about the niceties of fifteen centuries of liturgical usage, X people never go to church, except for the odd wedding or funeral. Furthermore, they don't know anyone who does go, and the whole idea would strike them as embarrassing. When obliged to bow their heads in prayer in public places, some X people have been known to raise their eyes surreptitiously to inspect the expressions, postures, and clothing of their more conformist neighbors. X people tend to make their own rules and to get away with so doing, which means that many of them are writers. And, as Diana Trilling has said, "If everyone . . . wants to be a writer, this is not only because of the promise of celebrity but also because of what the life of the artist promises of freedom to make one's own rules."

X people are verbal. They're good at languages and take it for granted that it is disgraceful, because merely American and provincial, to remain monolingual. Instead of the occasional dress-up foreign word of the middle and upper-middle classes (*gourmet*, *arrivederci*, *kaput*), Xs can deliver whole paragraphs in French, Italian, German, or Spanish, and sometimes Russian or Chinese as well. The more self-conscious Xs will sometimes go so far in the international direction as to cross their sevens. Soliciting no reputation for respectability, X people are freely obscene and profane, but tend to deploy vile language with considerable rhetorical effectiveness, differing from proles by using *fucking* as a modifier only now and then and never dropping the *g*. They may be rather fonder than most people of designating someone—usually a public servant or idol of the middle class—an *asshole*. This will suggest that generally they eschew euphemism, as, for example, when they insist that their children use the words *penis* and *vagina*. But they don't always call spades spades. Sometimes they will euphemize, but unlike more genteel speakers Xs like to use euphemisms ironically or parodically, favoring those especially which low newspapers use with a knowing, libel-skirting leer. Thus when an X person lifts one eyebrow slightly while referring to someone as a *confirmed bachelor*, we are to gather that *flaming homosexual* is meant. Similarly, as Neil Mackwood observes, *starlet* is the ironic euphemism for *whore*, *constant companion* for *lover*, *tired* (or *overtired*) for *publicly drunk*, and *fun-loving* for *promiscuous*. Applied to young women, *willowy* means *near death from anorexia*. X people can also use the middle class's euphemisms for sardonic effect if sufficient irony is signaled at the same time. Thus it is possible to speak of some poor soul's *kleptomania problem* in such a way as to install viciously skeptical quotation marks around the words.

Scrutinizing the British social classes over a century ago, Matthew Arnold identified the standard three and then observed that each class has in it people he termed *aliens*, those who feel they don't belong there and want out. It's largely from their current American counterparts that the X group is recruited. Some members, like Gore Vidal, enter from the upper class. Some, like James Jones, come from the proles, or even the destitute. One can have as little "education" as Jones, or as much as the brilliant kids from the more demanding universities who have developed confidence in their intellect and taste there. X people constitute something like a classless class. They occupy the one social place in the U.S.A. where the ethic of buying and selling is not all-powerful. Impelled by insolence, intelligence, irony, and spirit, X people have escaped out the back doors of those theaters of class which enclose others. And people fearful that X-hood may be somehow un-American should realize that, on the contrary, it is firmly in the American grain. Knowing that, Mark Twain created an exemplary category-X person and said when first introducing him, "Huckleberry came and went, at his own free will."

Although their places are not inheritable and although they lay little stress on manners, in their freedom X people constitute a sort of parody aristocracy. In some ways they resemble E. M. Forster's "aristocracy of the sensitive, the considerate, and the plucky," whose members are "sensitive for others as well as themselves,... considerate without being fussy." And "they can take a joke." "On they go," says Forster, warming to his vision, "an invincible army, yet not a victorious one":

> Authority, seeing their value, has tried to net them and to utilize them as the Egyptian Priesthood, or the Christian Church or the Chinese Civil Service or the Group Movement, or some other worthy stunt. But they slip through the net and are gone. . . .

If people with small imaginations and limited understandings aspire to get into the upper-middle class, the few with notable gifts of mind and perception aspire to disencumber themselves into X people. It's only as an X, detached from the constraints and anxieties of the whole class racket, that an American can enjoy something like the LIBERTY promised on the coinage. And it's in the X world, if anywhere, that an American can avoid some of the envy and ambition that pervert so many. De Tocqueville saw as early as 1845 what was likely to result from the official American reprehension of the aristocratic principle. "Desires still remain extremely enlarged," he wrote, "while the means of satisfying them are diminished day by day." And thus "on every side we trace the ravages of inordinate and unsuccessful ambition kindled in hearts which it consumes in secret and in vain." The society of Xs is not large at the moment. It could be larger, for many can join who've not yet understood that they have received an invitation.

❊❘ APPENDIX ❘❊

EXERCISES,
AND THE
MAIL BAG

EXERCISES

LEARNING TO DRAW CLASS
INFERENCES

(Answers at end of Exercise)

Indicate the class of each of the following:

1. A small girl who gives this account of her first visit to a symphony concert: "A waiter came out and tried to beat the band with a little stick."

2. A 50-year-old man on the deck of a 35-foot Chris-Craft, drinking from a can of Bud and attended by three luscious girls wearing halters and inexpensive white yachting caps.

3. A clean-cut young man on a plane. He's dressed in a three-piece dark suit, with a white shirt and conservative tie, and as he talks to his neighbor you can pick out words like *interface*, *funding*, *dialogue*, *lifestyle*, and *bottom line*.

4. A clean-cut young man on a plane. He's dressed in a three-piece dark suit, with a white shirt and conservative tie, and as he talks to his neighbor you can pick out words like *patina* (pronounced not just correctly but assertively and elegantly), *quattrocento*, and *the V and A*.

5. A young woman lawyer in a large New York firm who likes to watch Shakespeare on Educational Television and to frequent restaurants said to serve gour-

met food. "*The New Yorker* is practically my Bible," she says.

6. A middle-aged woman professor of classical epigraphy at a large and old East Coast university who spends her summers on digs in Anatolia and her winters copulating with a much younger boyfriend. Her mother was an orderly in a woman's prison, her father a high-school teacher of woodshop. Both were avid church-goers.

7. A man in his late twenties wearing three shirts at once. The undermost one is bright red, then there's a yellow one, and the one on top is a light-blue Oxford-cloth button-down.

8. A small-town barber whose wife is getting very fat.

9. A boy and girl in their twenties on a flight from New York to Los Angeles. They both wear dirty, raggedy jeans, and the boy's cotton shirt is faded and torn. Beneath her shirt you can clearly see her nipples. They both wear moccasins without soles, and without socks.

ANSWERS

(LEARNING TO DRAW CLASS INFERENCES)

1. This girl's class depends on the way the conductor was dressed. If he was in white tie, the girl's probably upper-class. If he was dressed otherwise, she's upper-middle—no little girls below upper-middle would be taken to the symphony.

2. He's a high prole, and he's saved all his life for that horrible boat. If he'll take the caps off the girls and pour his beer into a glass, he might pass for middle-class, or even upper-middle if he gets the girls into men's old shirts with the tails hanging out.

3. This guy's middle-class or even high-prole, a trainee with some hypertrophied corporation on his way to a "conference." He thinks he's giving off an upper-middle-class effect, but boy, is he wrong. He thinks he's going to be high in the company someday, but he's wrong there, too.

4. This guy's either upper-middle or upper. He's inherited some money, but he still enjoys doing a little work if it's appropriate—in his case, either part-time museum curatorship or light work in a gallery classy enough to deal in non-contemporary art. His friends will roll their eyes with astonishment if he ever marries.

5. She is hopelessly middle-class, and probably consumed with secret bitterness that she's not made upper-middle.

6. Category X, obviously, which makes the family background irrelevant, thrown in here merely as a smokescreen.

7. He is not insane, merely upper-middle-class displaying his command of layering. If he's stepped out of a very dirty old Chevrolet, he's probably upper-class.

8. He is barely a craftsman, but still he is one, and so he qualifies as a high prole. But if his wife gets much fatter, he will sink to mid-prole.

9. They are either upper-class or category X, engaged in the *épater-les-bourgeois* act of dressing way down for travel. If they were middle-class or prole they'd be dressed way up. Watch them closely. If they take off their moccasins and pad up and down the aisle in bare feet, they're probably category X. The nipples already argue category X.

THE LIVING-ROOM SCALE

(Revised)

(An early, primitive form of this was promulgated in 1935 by F. Stuart Chapin in his book *Contemporary American Institutions*.)

Begin with a score of 100. For each of the following in your living room (or those of friends or acquaintances) add or subtract points as indicated. Then ascertain social class according to the table at the end.

Hardwood floor	add 4
Parquet floor	add 8
Stone floor	add 4
Vinyl floor	subtract 6
Wall-to-wall carpet	add 2
Working fireplace	add 4
New Oriental rug or carpet	subtract 2 (each)
Worn Oriental rug or carpet	add 5 (each)
Threadbare rug or carpet	add 8 (each)
Ceiling ten feet high, or higher	add 6
Original paintings by internationally recognized practitioners	add 8 (each)

Original drawings, prints, or
   lithographs by internationally
   recognized practitioners   add 5 (each)
Reproductions of any Picasso
   painting, print, or anything   subtract 2 (each)
Original paintings, drawings, or
   prints by family members   subtract 4 (each)
Windows curtained, rods and
   draw cords   add 5
Windows curtained, no rods or
   draw cords   add 2
Genuine Tiffany lamp   add 3
Reproduction Tiffany lamp   subtract 4
Any work of art depicting
   cowboys   subtract 3
"Professional" oil portrait of any
   member of the household   subtract 3
Any display of "collectibles"   subtract 4
Transparent plastic covers on
   furniture   subtract 6
Furniture upholstered with any
   metallic threads   subtract 3
Cellophane on any lampshade   subtract 4
No ashtrays   subtract 2
Refrigerator, washing machine,
   or clothes dryer in living room subtract 6
Motorcycle kept in living room   subtract 10
Periodicals visible, laid out flat:
     National Enquirer   subtract 6
     Popular Mechanics   subtract 5
     Reader's Digest   subtract 3
     National Geographic   subtract 2
     Smithsonian   subtract 1
     Scientific American   subtract 1
     New Yorker   add 1
     Town and Country   add 2
     New York Review of Books add 5
     Times Literary Supplement
       (London)   add 5
     Paris Match   add 6
     Hudson Review   add 8

Each family photograph (black-and-white)	subtract 2
Each family photograph (color)	subtract 3
Each family photograph (black-and-white or color) in sterling-silver frame	add 3
Potted citrus tree with midget fruit growing	add 8
Potted palm tree	add 5
Bowling-ball carrier	subtract 6
Fishbowl or aquarium	subtract 4
Fringe on any upholstered furniture	subtract 4
Identifiable Naugahyde aping anything customarily made of leather	subtract 3
Any item exhibiting words in an ancient or modern foreign language (Spanish excluded)	add 7
Wooden venetian blinds	subtract 2
Metal venetian blinds	subtract 4
Tabletop obelisk of marble, glass, etc.	add 9
No periodicals visible	subtract 5
Fewer than five pictures on walls	subtract 5
Each piece of furniture over 50 years old	add 2
Bookcase(s) full of books	add 7
Any leather bindings more than 75 years old	add 6
Bookcase(s) partially full of books	add 5
Overflow books stacked on floor, chairs, etc.	add 6
Hutch bookcase ("wall system") displaying plates, pots, porcelain figurines, etc., but no books	subtract 4
Wall unit with built-in TV, stereo, etc.	subtract 4

On coffee table, container of
   matchbooks from funny or
   anomalous places   add 1

Works of sculpture (original, and
   not made by householder or
   any family member)   add 4 (each)

Works of sculpture made by
   householder or any family
   member   subtract 5 (each)

Every item alluding specifically
   to the United Kingdom   add 1

Any item alluding, even
   remotely, to Tutankhamen   subtract 4

Each framed certificate, diploma,
   or testimonial   subtract 2

Each "laminated" ditto   subtract 3

Each item with a "tortoiseshell"
   finish, if only made of
   Formica   add 1

Each "Eames chair"   subtract 2

Anything displaying the name or
   initials of anyone in the
   household   subtract 4

Curved moldings visible
   anywhere in the room   add 5

CALCULATING THE SCORE

245 and above	Upper class
185–245	Upper-middle
100–185	Middle
50–100	High prole
Below 50	Mid- or low prole

THE MAIL BAG

Dear Sir:

We are a young couple about to buy our first home. May we assume that a fireplace has more status than a garage?

The Hopefuls

Dear Hopefuls:

It does, but the garage shows: go for the garage. And don't say *home*—it's vulgar.

———

Dear Sir:

What about the class aspects of standing on the sidewalk in a large city and eating a hot dog or similar viand bought from a street peddler presiding over one of those little carts?

Puzzled

Dear Puzzled:

Only people very expensively dressed or terribly good-looking can do this without impairing their status. Middle-class people demean themselves further by doing this sort of thing, but uppers can confirm their high status by it, like appearing at an afternoon ball game in a costly suit, suggesting that you're doing the occasion honor. You also, in both activities, get high class-credit for your upper-class magnanimity in appearing to be democratic.

———

Dear Sir:

I am an Englishman planning to emigrate to the United States. Can you help me by explaining the class system there?

T. Atkins

Dear Mr. Atkins:

No, you'd never get it—much too complicated. You must be born and nurtured here. But you should have no worries, because here the fact of British birth raises your class at least one notch, no matter how nondescript and fourth-rate you may in fact be.

———

Dear Sir:

Is the metric system vulgar?

Anxious

Dear Anxious:

A complicated question. To the degree that the metric system deviates from older British usages, it is rather vulgar. But then too, insofar as it evokes French and even Italian practices, it has a certain panache, as in "I'd like a half-kilo of that nice-looking *ris de veau*." I think it finally depends on what you measure with it. Knowing how much a liter is, after all, identifies you immediately as a person long intimate with the contents of imported wine bottles.

———

Dear Sir:

I have been living in Georgetown for thirty years and find I must move to Del Rio, Texas. Will I suffer a loss of caste?

Nervous

Dear Nervous:

How can you ask? You'll never be able to show your face in civilized company again. But at least you're not moving to Miami.

———

Dear Sir:

To settle a bet, would you indicate some things that are vulgar?

Curious

Dear Curious:

I'd say these are vulgar, but in no particular order: Jerry Lewis's TV telethon; any "Cultural Center"; Beef Wellington; cute words for drinks like *drinky-poos* or *nightcaps*; dinner napkins with high polyester content; colored wineglasses; oil paintings depicting members of the family; display of laminated diplomas. On the other hand, these things are not vulgar: fireworks on the Fourth of July; sirloin steaks; paper napkins; old clothes. You should be able to infer the principle and go on from there.

———

Dear Sir:

I play a carillon in a church tower. Someone I know says that carillons are lower in class than regular church bells. Is he right?

Ringer

Dear Ringer:

I'm afraid he is. But some of the status weakness can be mitigated by playing nice things, like, say, "Melody in F" instead of "Annie Laurie," "The Old Gray Mare," or "The Impossible Dream." Since your letter does not come from Southern California, I assume you actually push the handles rather than play an amplified tape very loud. If you're terribly worried about your status, you should seek another line of work. And try to find acquaintances who are more tactful.

———

Dear Sir:

My son attends Eckerd College in St. Petersburg, Florida, but he insists on putting a Harvard sticker in the rear window of his car. Is this wrong?

Worried

Dear Worried:

It is very wrong, but at least it indicates that he's learning something down there. He may go far.

———

Dear Sir:

My bank teller embarrasses me terribly by saying at the end of the transaction, "Have a nice day." I don't know what I'm supposed to say back. Can you help?

Sincere

Dear Sincere:

I suppose you can say "You too" or "Have one yourself," although this last, like "Have one on me," would sound a bit flippant. You should never say "Mind your own business"—that would be very rude.

The best response to "Have a nice day," I think, is the one devised by a British friend of mine. He says:

"Thank you, but I have other plans." Perfectly polite, and yet it leaves no doubt that you are *not* in that person's social class.

ABOUT THE AUTHOR

Paul Fussell is Donald T. Regan Professor of English at the University of Pennsylvania and author of many books on eighteenth-century and modern British culture. His book THE GREAT WAR AND MODERN MEMORY won the National Book Award in 1976 together with the National Book Critics Circle Award and the Ralph Waldo Emerson Award from Phi Beta Kappa. His more recent books are ABROAD: *British Literary Traveling Between the Wars* and THE BOY SCOUT HANDBOOK AND OTHER OBSERVATIONS, a collection of essays from a wide range of British and American magazines. He has taught at Connecticut College, the University of Heidelberg, and, for twenty-eight years, at Rutgers University. Mr. Fussell has lectured widely at universities here and abroad. He publishes literary criticism in *Harper's* and the *New Republic*, both of which he serves as a contributing editor.